Mastery of Hunting

Mastery of Hunting

Quality Outdoor Gear Products
CLICK HERE

CAMPING WORLD
America's RV And Outdoor Store

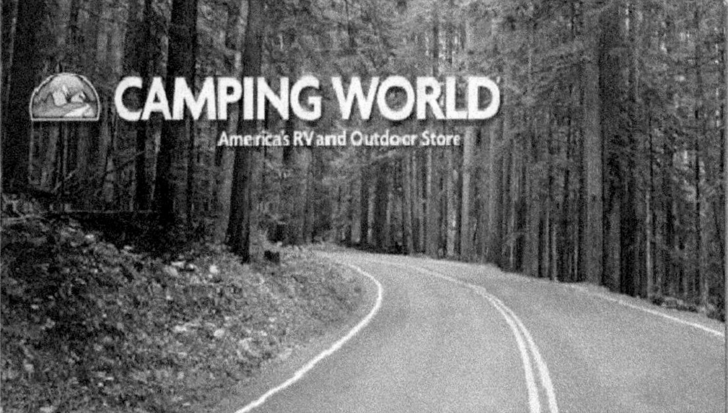

CAMPING WORLD
America's RV and Outdoor Store
Anything And Everything
To Do With Camping!
Get all the products to make your
next family camping trip more enjoyable.
Find huge discounts on the best camping
equipments!
Providing Quality Camping Gear Since 1966

CAMPING
WORLD
INTERNET
ONLY
SPECIALS
SAVE
UP TO
40%
CLICK FOR
DETAILS

CAMPING WORLD
America's RV And Outdoor Store

Mastery of Hunting

Contents

Deer Hunting Tips

Deer hunting is an interesting thing that reminds you of those golden old ages of 19th centuries, where a handsome hunk well equipped with all hunting material rides on horse searching for his target animal either for the purpose of displaying his masculine powers or for enticing and wooing his lady love. Sounds interesting and fascinating? Yes it is! But unfortunately, gone are those days. However, even when deer hunting is carried out these days; it happens to be an amusing and entertaining experience.

Successful deer hunting doesn't require much of a deliberated effort on the part of the hunter. Rather, if few simple tips and things are kept in mind, it would certainly make it a triumphant adventure. So, now pack up your bags and get ready to play the exciting game of hunting deer without any extra ado.

Timing

Time is one of the chief factors to be kept in mind before leaving for deer hunting. The best time to bag a deer are sunsets and sunrise. This is because the lightning at these times confuses the sight of deer and you can see herd of this poor animal looking for its food for the purpose of filling its empty stomach. These timings also ensure the safety of your teammates. You can also start as early as possible before sunrise by hiding yourself in safe places. This way you can easily pounce upon your required variety as sun rises, without getting noticed by them.

Things to avoid

If you think your most expensive perfume will aid you in catching your prey, then think again. It would be better, if you avoid any kind of perfumes, after shaves, colognes or any kind of sturdy scented fragrance. Try to keep the artificial smells to minimum. Before leaving for deer hunting, try to blend the smell of your body with countryside, otherwise the smell of human body may deteriorate your purpose of deer hunting. You can always try out these expensive and powerful smelling deodorants after you are finished up with your deer hunting.

Silence: the best guiding factor

Keeping mum considerably increase your chances of deer finding. Though deer hunting may be a fun-packed and amusing experience for you and your friends, you need to take care of the noise factor. Deer remain quite cautious about sound. This is the most important tip to be kept in mind while driving for deer hunting; otherwise you will end up losing that prized buck.

These few simple basic tips, if kept in mind, will result in a better deer hunting experience; a memorable amusing and enjoyable adventure not only for you, but for your team mates too. So what are you waiting for? Get, set and go on your hunting spree.

Deer Hunting: Watching Deer In Your Backyard

Now, all of you must be waiting for the deer to come into your backyard so that you can nicely watch them. There is a possibility that you can also hunt them. But, how is this dream possible? It is possible by only one way. That way is to put feeders in your backyard or a specific hunting position. Here are some more important tips to magnetize the deer at your location.

Deer Feeders- A great way

If you are hunting, deer feeders are the best way to bring deer to your spot. You should make it a point that deer are fed on acorns. Mostly, you should hunt in the fall season as there are good numbers of oak trees. Put a feeder a bit away from the deer, if there are not so good numbers of oak trees. Also, you can find some deer droppings around a few trees. Try and try till you succeed, who knows you eventually might get lucky.

Also, if possible, try to protect the feeder from leaves and rains. Further, you can offer good supply of water near the feeder. This will help as the deer will fall into the trap of deer feeder, while drinking water.

Catching a Glimpse of Deer Feeding

It is indeed stunning to watch deer feeding from your house. You can watch it through your Kitchen window or the living room. Make use of a normal and routine feeder and combine some rice or corn in it. If that does not work out well with the deer, put apples in the feeder or else, place the feeder near some water. Also, you can place some peanut butter on some nearby trees.

These varieties of food are a great attraction for the deer. Once the deer falls into your attraction, your work is done. Also, if there are some cows around your area, make use of some rice variety rather than using corn variety as cows generally do not prefer eating rice.

Moreover, you should always keep a close watch on your feeder as there are chances of other animals rather than deer to get attracted to your feeder.

Walking the nature photographer's dream

Which natural view in nature could be better than a deer feeding sight? If you are an avid fan of nature and are longing to take a snap of deer feeding sight, it is possible if you follow some few tips:

1. Be far from the deer so that it is not able to hear or even notice that someone is trying to take a snap.
2. Use a good lens which has an extra large zoom, so that you won't have any problem while taking a snap of the deer from a long distance.
3. Locate the feeder in such a location where the deer won't get scared after encountering with the feeder.
4. Make use of some beautiful backyards so that after looking at the snaps, you feel the thrill of nature's beauty.

Deer Hunting: About Axis Deer

If you are wondering about hunting the breed of axis deer, you can take a look over numerous ranches placed throughout the state of Texas. Axis deer, known for their large horns, fall under the most favorable hunting category for hunters. Axis deer form the top class breed amongst the other type of deer breeds, thus providing the best meat among all wild breed deer.

About axis deer

Hunters find the bodies of these axis deer quite appealing and striking. The body spots of these axis deer find a resemblance and blends finely with its natural environments featured by thickly layered forest and scrub brushes. Hunting an axis deer is a challenging and thrilling task, which tempts the hunters to pursue it at any moment of the year. On an average, the length of antlers on these deer ranges from two to two and a half feet, if measured lengthwise. Hunters find it very eye-catching and feel like having one of such breed in their hunting adventure. Sometimes, a hunter who strikes on such trophy quality deer appears delightful and pleasantry surprised on finding the antlers size of three feet.

Axis deer are known as natural fighters and have left behind the category of Bengal tigers in their native land of Sri Lanka only. This quality of axis deer excites the people to carry outhunting of these special kinds of deer on regular basis. Axis deer shed their antlers on regular intervals, thus their left out antlers pave the way for their hunters quest by prompting and inciting them. There are no proper schedules or fixed measures with which hunters can determine the deer's antler transformation.

Don't get demoralized

You will notice that axis deer always stay in herds and very rarely move in single. It may be quite frightening for some and demoralizing for some. Guys, if you really wish to catch your prey make sure you are skillful in various techniques of hunting but at the same time; work in a very human way. Axis deer is a very smart social animal that knows very well about the way of building the best alarm systems around themselves, so that it can help him in times of danger. They bellow and bawl in order to warn its fellow deer about danger.

Hunters need to take proper steps in order to have an axis deer in their side; otherwise all the efforts for hunting this sturdy and brawny minded deer will be in vain. The absolute and sheer size of axis deer makes them quite appealing among hunters hunting list. Thus, to conclude, we can say that if these simple minor things are kept in mind then efforts made in respect of hunting an axis deer will surely get you fruitful results.

Deer Hunting: Alabama Deer Hunting

If you are dreaming about hunting a white tail deer, then Alabama is the best place to be looked into. It does not matter, if you are an aspiring hunter or a well-experienced hunting champ. Alabama offers the best ambience for catching your prey. Here, you can easily hunt in well-managed properties specially designed for hunting purposes. It offers you to choose between bow and a gun for your hunting adventure.

No matter you are amateur or well experienced; you'll surely have great time hunting in Alabama farms. This place provides you a wonderful opportunity of hunting white tail deer, which is the most familiar species of deer, found in south. Alabama offers you an area of more than 5000 acres of land for hunting purpose, where you can easily found a good number of deer population.

Recent developments

It is quite rewarding to know that the amount of money generated and quantity of hunting activity, both have tremendously increased in Alabama. Alabama has increasing prospects of deer hunting today. Also some of well-established farms provide deer hunting classes in winters in wooded areas. This sounds amazing and fascinating, right?

In Alabama, you can choose amongst the wide variety of pastures or hunting lands according to your suitability and desirability. You also have an option of choosing from guided hunts or from your self- assessed hunting understanding.

Time factor

This may sound as a shortcoming as deer hunting in Alabama is seasonal in nature. You just can't walk into woods seeking for your trophy deer at any moment of time. It is very important to take the timing factor in notice, before packing bags for hunting adventure in Alabama. You also need to check with relevant authorities regarding the same.

Favorable months

Mid October is the best time for bow hunting in Alabama. For gun hunting, you need to wait until November ends. Even the dates are not fixed; you need to contact the concerned authorities and should go through schedules of hunting season from Alabama wildlife department.

Alabama deer hunting is getting quite popular. Many enthusiastic and passionate white tail deer hunters have started residing in nearby places in Alabama. Deer hunting in proper season gives one rewarding results as they can have an eye on number of prey target.
As Alabama provides number of hunting opportunities with minimal restrictions, it proves to be a very profitable business option for state.

Deer Hunting: Finding The Perfect Location

Deer hunting is an art. You need to have a perfect place to hunt a deer, probably a perfect tree stand. Some tips which help you to hunt a deer can really be helpful to find a perfect spot for getting a deer down.

Basic Preparation

For hunting a deer, you need to know that where the deer actually reside. The preparation for finding a deer location should begin at least three to four weeks in advance. Catching a deer location before that might not really help as they might have changed their routes.

However, you can keep a few areas where deer can be found in your mind and may be re-consider and re-evaluate those areas while actually going for hunting.

Care should be exercised in making minimal changes to the surroundings and leaving little, or if possible, no signs of you being there. After finding the perfect spot, place your tree stand over there. This is done to get the deer used to seeing that stand at that location.

Choosing multiple sites can be helpful as this might leave little scent behind.

Checking for the food source

Awareness in terms of the food that deer eat during the season for hunting can be helpful. Trees that are producing nuts start dropping the nuts while the hunting season starts. Therefore once can track the deer foot-prints by finding out areas where hickory or nuts or acorns are dropped around. Other food items such as mushrooms, farm crops, herbs, apples, grass etc are also consumed by deer. Trailing these foods can help you find a deer location.

Rest Domains

One should also check for the rejuvenating and sleeping areas of deer. Generally they sleep in areas where there are thick bushes. Also find the trails where the deer move for feeding their child. These areas might be at a distance and off the track. Larger bucks normally go beyond the normal areas into further deeper brushes.

Their sign might not be seen into some most common trails. These large bucks follow the common trail only while they go up for feed.

Problems Faced

- Boring as you have to wait for the deer to appear
- High chances of you dosing off to sleep while waiting for the deer
- Making unnecessary sounds and noises or movement due to uneasiness

Solutions

- Make yourself comfortable by coming out of the tree stand whenever you feel uneasy
- Set up heat and motion detectors at the deer trails, using a deer trail monitoring system. These can alert you whenever the deer is approaching you

Thus, these tips can help you select a perfect location and have a nice hunting season with deer.

Deer Hunting: Hunting Mule Deer

Mule Deer are normally found in the Western US Region in bachelor groups. They are also found in southern western of Saskatchewan and are at time also spotted in Minnesota and Missouri. Mule Deer are very adaptable to most kinds of terrain. Regions providing low water and nutrition content are normally devoid of mule deer.

Description

Mule deer have very large mule like ears. Their color is reddish-brown in the summer while in winter it turns to grayish-brown. They also have white patches in the body in belly, throat, and nose eye and ear areas. Black spots as well can be found on the chin. They have a white tail which ending in black.

Special Features

- Mule like ears give them an ability to listen sharply
- Binocular vision. however cannot detect motionless objects
- Good runner and swimmers

Living habits

Eating: They are normally gazers and eat green plants, nuts and corn, and herbs.
Lifestyle: They foray into deep valleys and bushy fields. However, after feeding and watering themselves, they move to the areas where their beds are. Their beds are normally in the areas located on ridge slopes, rocky areas, bushy areas or areas with timber work. The selection of their sleeping area or bed areas thus looks to be dependent upon having enough support for their back. They also want to be in little higher regions so as to keep a watch on the approaching predators. This makes it difficult for us to locate them.

Tracks: The track of mule deer varies depending upon the landscape. In softer and woodland areas, their foot print is a little pointed whereas on harder ground the print has a blunt tip.

Main Predators for Mule Deer

- Mountain Lion and Coyotes in the Nevada region
- Other predators include black bear, grizzly Bear, wolves and any human animal

Hunting Mule Deer

For a bow hunter: You should try spot and stalk style of hunting; although it is difficult, it is not impossible. All that you would require is a collection of proper optical glasses, binoculars and a spotting scope. You should scan the areas like high ridges, pockets in mountains and brushes where mule deer are most likely to be found. Scan the high ridges, brush pockets and rock outcroppings.

After locating a buck of your interest, you should start working on your plan. Since these mule deer are in higher terrains, you will have to use breaks in order to install your stalk. The best way is to surprise the animal from upper area. Successful stalk gives good opportunity for hunt. For a running buck wait for it to stop and then try the stalk.

To summarize, one should always be patient while hunting.

Deer Hunting: Deer Hunting Blinds

Initially, blinds were just used as a cover device for the hunters to protect them from getting detected by the animals. Deer hunting blinds helped in locating deer hidden in the cliff area.

Deer hunting blinds is a commercial product easily available in the market place. These are also placed in deer hunting grounds and at different farms so that hunters can use them along with the other facilities of staying and lodging built over there in the form of a cabin.

Hunting deer in neighborhood-Prefabricated sets

Deer can be hunted in the backyard of your house as well. However, the problem is only related with the inability to hide properly in the woods. Also, we tend to leave our scent behind in the hunting ground. These situations can be avoided by using proper hunting blinds. Pre fabricated hunting blinds are easily available in the market. Construction sets available in the market also help to build your own blind by setting the angle and height.

These sets can be easily disassembled and again be assembled to make it ready as a blind. You should look for steel brackets so as to assure that they are strong enough and can provide you enough safety.

Check

While using a hunting blind just ensure that these hunting blinds are properly assembled. Disassembly instructions should also be carefully followed by you so as to leave you with no further questions on the safety aspect. While buying any such device, safety should be the top most priority. Cost concerns should be ignored as inexpensive units might ultimately lead you to loss.

Deer hunting blinds should be able to meet all the basic requirements of the hunter without causing any troubles. This does not mean that they are to be luxurious or should have excellent aesthetic features. The color should be simple to mix with the color of woods and trees and that is all that is required.

Important Elements of Blind

One should be able to set up blinds in very little time, so that movement from one spot to other is easily possible. The most important thing that is required while sitting in a blind is the visibility. It is your ability to see a deer from different sides of the blind that is important. Moreover, the deer should not be able to see you. Many prefabricated blinds are available which can provide you these features without having letting to pay you any extra money for this.

Deer blinds might not be allowed legally at all the places. Therefore a hunter should check the laws before using any such device. Simply sitting at a standstill at a tree base is anyway permitted in all the regions where hunting is legal.

Deer Hunting: Whitetail Deer

Are you too worried about how to get whitetail deer into your trap like everyone else? If yes, then you have a reason to be relieved of your worries, because you are going to be equipped with some amazing tips, which will help you to be successful in hunting whitetail deer. It may be really irritating and frustrating; when you see the deer escape from you in a jiffy, whereas you cannot do anything about it. Is that not true? Another fact is that the escape of the deer in front of your eyes is the most sudden disappearing acts in the natural world till now. Have you ever given a little thought as to how to tackle this problem or what is the factor that is causing the problem? If given a thought, then you will find that the answer is your odor or smell.

You will be surprised to know that the slightest odor of you can make the deer alert. The reason behind this is that the deer are actually gifted with the senses which help them to identify or recognize the human odor. They can not only identify the smell but also the noises of the slightest movements. So, while on the verge of hunting a deer, one should move forward without making an inch of noise. Else, you are bound to play hide and seek with the deer, thus making it very difficult to capture it.

If you are hunting with any kind of weapon, then smell reduction is always wanted and quite longing. But, if you are hunting with any kind of hand gun or bow, then smell reduction is of supreme importance. Also, you would like to go closer and closer to the deer, when you are equipped with such weapons. But then, it is important to keep yourself from smell. Now the question is how is it possible? What you can do is that you can buy some very good smell reduction products available in market and apply those on your body before going to fight the battle. But, if proper planning is done systematically with the product, you can get the better of the dilemma. Also, you should be self confident about yourself as it is very important.

Wind factor is another essential factor in combating the problem. The region where you are expecting the deer should be upwind from your location. The best way is to make the animal get placed in such a way that it is upwind or crosswind from our location. Try having many stand locations, so that wind direction would not be a matter of concern. You will always be in a downwind position to attack the deer. Also, be calm, patient and wait for the most favorable wind to come across your way. Then, only take the plunge. Thus, if you plan in a constructive way, there is no reason why you could not struck a boat out of the blue.

Deer Hunting: Texas Style

If you go to Texas, you will find out that there are a large number of deer hunter fanatics out there, who just love to hunt deer. It is a very routine kind of a thing there. Also, do you know that Texas is the second largest place in the nation to comprise of deer hunters? In Texas, there are a large number of deer available and all of different sizes and breeds. Even though, deer are in large numbers, many are discontented as they are allowed to hunt only a small number of deer.

But, to increase the popularity of deer hunting among out of the state people, hunting on land owned by private owners is permitted. A price is quoted for those who want to hunt on a private land by the owners themselves.

But, in order to do so, a license is needed for the land owner too to give access to others to hunt in their land. Also, to Texas residents, if they want to hunt in some wildlife parks or some national parks, though it is permitted, a license is required for hunting. You are bound to go behind the bars if you are not having a license. As Texas is such a large state, laws are strictly put into effect and also are quite stringent.

People who are interested in hunting can walk their dream in many ways. Often, they accompany their friends along to the hunting place and have a ball out there. Also, there are guides available for new people to Texas. If you are lucky enough, you can come back home with a deer trophy in your hand. But, not anybody can participate in hunting. It is quite necessary to pass a safety hunting course, which is put into effect by the authorities, if you want to participate in the competitions.

There is another way also to enter this adventurous competition. It is a lottery system implemented to bring more and more people into deer hunting, which are mostly applicable for a span of ten days. So, if your fate is walking with you, you can be chosen for the competition. During the season of the competition, many people come to see it. The whole competition area is flooded with audiences desperate to catch a glimpse. Texas Department of Wildlife says that more than 1.3 million is produced at the time of the season and that too in a year. It is advisable that you plan and book your hotel as soon as possible, if you are planning to go to Texas for a deer hunting journey. It is likely that no hotels will be available, if the schedule is delayed.

The money generated from the competition goes into conservation of the wildlife. Thus, it will be indeed a great experience to see the deer hunting programs in Texas.

Deer Hunting: Aggravation Or Alleviation

Do you know that deer hunting is the most famous in the United States of America? One reason behind this is that they are available plentiful in the country. But, it is indeed not so easy to hunt the deer as they also make use of tricks. Also, a deer does not behave the same way every time. According to weather, mating season and time of day, they change their behavioral characteristics. A good hunter will know what behavior the deer is fitted into in a specific type of season. In the United States of America, one can hunt in public or private grounds only if one obeys some strict laws enforced, which say that you should have a license to hunt. Moreover, one should obey the rules and regulations of the season very strictly.

It is not easy to be a hunter. You should pass the hunter safety test in order to qualify for the hunting competition or season. They come out of their hiding places just moments before dusk and dawn. Hunters get only thirty minutes to implement their hunting skills before sunrise and after sunset. Moon also plays an important role in controlling the movement of the deer. A good hunter will always know about the various moon cycles and how they are going to affect the deer as it will be quite essential for hunting. Also, hunters are aware of what time is the sun going to set and what time is the sun going to rise. This travelling just daylight and twilight is because of the fact that deer are nocturnal animals. If one does not know about all these factors, he is bound to get so irritated and frustrated that he may give up his idea of hunting due to bad outcome.

Moreover, another advantage that deer has over human beings is that they are gifted with the sense of identifying smell or odor in a jiffy. Also, they have very good hearing abilities and can be aware of some danger even if a slightest noise is made. So, one has to be extra careful while on the hunting venture for deer. Moreover, deer come out of their hiding places, when they feel hungry or they hear some sort of sound of winds or rains etc. But, the hunter has to be lucky enough to be on his toes when the deer is out.

Mostly, it is said that fall mating season is the best for hunting. It is very ordinary to see deer out in the center of the daytime in this season, which is actually the time to take a nap for the deer during other seasons. This is because during this season, their behavior is quite uncommon. So, the opportunities escalate during this season for the hunters.

Thus, hunting can be a great pleasure if you are victorious in it. Else, it can also be a matter of aggravation.

Deer Hunting: Alabama

Alabama is one of the best places for the seasoned or novice deer hunter, especially if you seriously into hunting whitetail deer. Alabama laws permit you to use either bow or gun when hunting so this is another good choice for you since most other states have restrictions in this respect. Novice hunters will be interested in the several deer farms and preserves that can ensure a great hunting time in Alabama. There are a number of farms and lodges in Alabama that are especially well suited for those looking to hunt for whitetail deer, which incidentally happens to be the most common species of deer in the south. The hunting properties are quite large in Alabama and may cover up to 5000 acres of land area and have a rich deer population.

Another bit of good news for deer hunters visiting Alabama is that in the past few years the ratio of large bucks to does has gone up quite dramatically. There are also some farms in Alabama that offer winter classes in order to train novice hunters in deer hunting in the most heavily wooded areas.

The preserves in Alabama are used for a wide variety of purposes. The one that is right for you depends on your hunting goals. For example you may prefer to hunt in open tracts rather than wooded areas for small bucks and does. These preserves come with specially designated areas where hunters may search for that trophy buck. You may also opt for self-assessed hunting or guided hunts. Also keep in mind that the deer hunting in Alabama is seasonal. This means that there are only specific times of the year that are ideal for deer hunting. So you cannot plan you trip whenever you wish without first checking the season. It is always best to call up your destination and speak to someone experienced before starting to pack for that hunting trip.

The bow hunting season starts around the middle of October while the gun hunting season begins towards the end of November. The Alabama Department of Wildlife publishes the exact dates every year so it is best to check with them as the dates are not the same every year.

Alabama is getting increasingly popular with deer hunters. Keen deer hunters have been moving to Alabama to enjoy this sport while others are very regular visitors. Just remember to pick the right time to visit Alabama for deer hunting.

Deer Hunting: Kansas

The hunting season in Kansas begins when the green forests turn to a blazing orange. The Kansas deer hunting season begins in the fall every year and more than $22 billion is spent during this time. The expense goes towards the purchase of clothing, including the specially made head-to-foot blaze orange, guns with powerful scopes, ammunition, travel, and accommodation to stay in the woods when looking for the trophy white tail buck.

The winning prize in Kansas deer hunting belongs with the largest antlers. Kansas is believed to be the best hunting location for atypical whitetail deer. The state has a certificate of Trophy for all hunters who achieve a certain minimum score with deer. In order to win the certificate you must get more than 17 inches of antlers or horns of a white tail buck.

Most of the hunting grounds in Kansas are privately owned. For those parts that are not privately owned there are guides that help hunters to find the right spot where they may hunt. The hunting land in Kansas is made of creek and river bottoms, cedar and hardwood draws, and CPR fields. Majority of the crop fields grow corn, Milo, wheat alfalfa, and soybean. Northern Central Kansas has the richest soil in the entire state. Acorns are a large crop from which the Kansas whitetail deer gets a lot of nutrients. In Eastern Kansas you will find the larger whitetail deer. Most of the land is flat in Kansas with small wooded regions meaning the deer have fewer hiding places. They tend to travel in herds because of this.

Bow hunting season in Kansas begins in September and lasts till the gun hunting season begins. There are two rifle hunting seasons in Kansas, end of November and start of December. You need to have hunter education if your date of birth is later than 1 July, 1957. This is represented through the card that you must carry at all times when hunting. You also need to have a permit for deer hunting. There are only a limited number of permits granted every year through draws. The license permits hunters to hunt for small game and birds. This license is only valid for a calendar year and not the hunting season.

Deer hunting in Kansas requires proper attention to safety and the right hunting techniques. These procedures and techniques are taught during the hunting education course that most hunters nowadays are required to attend.

Deer Hunting: Texas

Texas is quite popular with deer hunters because of the large population available for hunting and also because of the size of the deer. Whitetail and mule deer can both be found in several locations across the large state of Texas. Most out-of-state hunters visiting Texas are quite often disappointed with the fact that only a few of them are permitted to hunt in the state. The reason for this is that the residents of Texas are second in America for the number of people that hunt deer in their state. The only workaround for this as far as out of state deer hunters are concerned is to rely on private land owners who often allow them to hunt on their property for a set fee.

There are many parks and wildlife areas in Texas that are frequented for hunting purposes. You need a license to hunt in Texas. If caught hunting without one, you may be fined or even imprisoned for having violated the state laws. Because Texas is a large state the hunting laws are enforced very strictly. Even private land owners offering hunting services to out-of-state hunters need a license allowing them to use their land for such a purpose.

You can hunt in Texas in several different ways. You can either go on a solo adventure or you can travel with friends. There are also some good guided tours that cover the best hunting grounds in Texas. Texas offers the highest probability for a hunter to come back with a trophy. However, you must demonstrate that you have successfully finished the hunter's safety course before you can participate in Texas deer hunting. A lottery system is used to decide who qualifies to get the deer hunting tag. Most of these tags are only valid for 10 days.

The deer hunting season in Texas is a very busy time. The Texas Department of Wildlife reports that over $1.3 million is spent every year on deer hunting. This includes the cost of deer tags, hunting equipment, accommodation, food, and other shopping. Because of the heavy rush it is best to plan a Texas hunting trip early on to avoid problems late in the season. Finding accommodation can become quite troublesome later on. A lot of the money generated through deer hunting is directed towards wildlife conservation. The Wildlife Restoration Program is constantly monitoring the number of animals in Texas. Because of the huge population of deer they are allowed to be hunted instead of being left to die of starvation.

Deer Hunting: Whitetail Deer

One of the most common experiences shared among whitetail deer hunters it the mystery of the sudden disappearance of a deer in range. Every hunter has been through it a few times. You are sitting perfectly still in a perfect spot and that perfect trophy buck enters into range. You hold your breath and are about to do the needful when the animal suddenly snaps to attention and in the blink of an eye does a quick about-turn and vanishes. The most common reason for this happening is the hunter's scent.

What makes whitetail deer hunting challenging is that these deer come with hypersensitivity for danger. They sense of sight and smell in simply amazing. If you move around even a little bit or there is even the slightest unnatural sound coming from your location then you can forget about a successful hunt. The same result may be expected if you barge into the woods without factoring in human scent. You may as well be announcing your arrival through a powerful amplifier and flashing lights.

Even the tiniest hint of human smell means the deer, regardless of age, sex, or size, is going to go shooting away before you know what is happening. It is desirable to reduce your scent as much as possible regardless of the sort of weapon you are using though it becomes extremely crucial when hunting with a bow or handgun. Hunting with either of these means that you have to remain undetected to get close enough for a proper shot. There are several scent reduction products available today but even with them you cannot completely remove all scent. However, they are still good tools in the hunter's arsenal because through they may not cause complete scent elimination they do go a long way in reducing it. You simply need to mix some common sense along with these products to get that extra edge when you are hunting for whitetail deer.

Wind direction plays a key role in staying undetected when hunting. Deer must always be upwind from your position otherwise you will be detected long before you even set eyes on one. You may as well spend the day in the library for the deer you will see if they are to your downwind. If you have troubles keeping them downwind then try to keep them in a crosswind. Good hunters have more than one stand so that they can change their position no matter what the wind direction.

Deer Hunting: A Short Hoof

Deer hunting is among the most popular among all forms of hunting. One reason for this is that the United States has a healthy deer population but the real reason is that they are very sensitive animals that change their behavior depending on time of the day, the weather, the mating season, and so on. The result is that deer present the hunter with a challenge like no other animal.

Deer hunting requires the hunter to all the factors affecting the animal's behavior singly, all at once, or any combination that may result from the environment. Deer hunting can be conducted with the bow or with the rifle.

Different states have their own regulations and laws for deer hunting and you must pay attention to them to avoid prosecution. Hunting may happen on public or private hunting grounds depending on various factors.

Unlike herbivores deer tend to be nocturnal. This is because their travels between feeding areas take place between sunrise and sunset. Most hunting grounds give hunters half an hour after dusk or before dawn to hunt for deer. As with most nocturnal animals the moon has considerable affect on their behavior. A good hunter knows that this should also be factored into the game plan. You need to know the correct time for sunrise and sunset and you also need to know the cycles of the moon during hunting season. Success at deer hunting is not something you can have at your convenience. If you plan to go hunting when you feel like it then you are only going to meet frustration.

Even if you are not a hunter you should be aware that deer are well known for their keen sense of danger. Deer have excellent sense of sight, smell, and sound.

Even the sound of snow falling on the ground is enough to set them running. This is why even the best camouflage does not work with deer because they can easily smell predators. Deer hunters prefer stands built on trees as the best place to stay away from the hypersensitivity of deer.

The fall mating season is preferred by some deer hunters because deer behavior during mating season tends to be incautious. Mating season lasts for around a month and hunters can be seen frequenting hunting grounds because their job is a lot easier at this time. It is also the only time when bucks and does can be seen during mid-day because aside from the mating season the mid-day is the resting period for deer.

Elk Hunting With A Bow

Elk are big animals in size. Many hunters don't believe the truth about the size of Elk until they see it actually.

You must be very good shooter for doing well at archery elk hunt. The things which one need to know about elk is habits of elk, its dwelling place, its place of feeding, its eating and drinking habits etc. The foremost thing, which one needs to do for archery elk hunting, is to gain complete understanding about the animal.

You need to establish your camp at a place where there is availability of source of fresh water. The animal will surely pay visit to its place of fresh drinking water sooner or later in case you keep on waiting for the animal at that place. The animals will also pay a visit to nearest area where large numbers of trees are available near their dwelling place.

Elk eat on grass and some kinds of berries. The types of berries include strawberries, blackberries and snowberries. Your first step for hunting elk should be to search for sources of food. The elk will come to place of availability of their food.

You can establish a set up on the earth or on a tree. You have to spend a lot of time on this set up for verifying that this set up is comfortable and everything which you require is available on it. You should try to establish many set ups and keep on changing your place. The smells of human beings remain at a place for many days and elk will not prefer to visit such places.

You also require a bow that is packed with a substantial punch. The arrows, which you use for shooting, should be large enough to make an uncontaminated kill. You need a great practice for developing skill of making good shots.

You should wear same device during practice session for shooting, which you are going to wear during hunting of elk. There is great difference between shooting a bow in a simple t shirt and shooting a bow while you are wrapped in heavy coats and disguise. The difference between this is same as difference between a successful shot and an unsuccessful shot.

Some hunters use a method of cow call or the method of bugling while archery elk hunting as these methods work more efficiently while hunting. These methods are very good when the animals are in heat and groove.

Many hunters prefer the use of cow call method. Archery elk hunting is a very complex task. Elks are very big animals and you should have a good a very good shot. You should learn the important part of archery elk hunting.

Elk Hunting: Packing

The elk hunting is gaining fuel as the adventurous sport in various regions of the world. One needs to plan before hand to make this adventurous sport a lifelong experience that remains in your memory for long time.

The guides and other concerned authorities may provide you with the list of the stuff you should carry along with you.

However, you are required to make some plans yourself. The foremost plan is regarding the choice of the place you want to visit, as different hunting places have different requirements.

For instance, Michigan, as a deer hunting ground requires different set of accessories than the elk hunting grounds of Ozark.

Carry Out A Smart Research

If you are the first time visitor to a particular hunting site, you need to acquire a handful of information. This information could be achieved from the smart research on the Internet.

You may find the information regarding the favorable part of the year to visit the place along with the weather conditions of the place. You may also want to know about the wildlife available there.

There are official websites maintained by the concerned authorities of different places, which help you in tones about the conditions prevailing in a particular region.

Then, you can prepare according to the needs of the place.

Gather The Basic Hunting Accessories

It is advisable to pack the various accessories related to hunting in your luggage with great care. Always take along the perfect hunting rifles, along with the fair amount of bullets.

You may also pack the sidearm in your hunter bags. Don't forget to pack the kit for cleaning the hunting rifles. A rifle with scope should be accompanied with lens brushes.

Now, about the personal accessories, you are required to accommodate the sleeping bags along with the space blanket. The space blanket, that is very easy to pack, saves your body heat in the cold weather.

This is a very essential requirement in the case you are lost from your hunting group, as it is coated with a special material that traps your body heat and doesn't allow it to move out.

Some Other Things To Pack

The clothes should be packed with respect to the weather condition during day as well as night. Also, one must take the basic first aid to get helped in case of minor injuries.

Never forget to take enough supply of eatables to avoid the shortage. It is recommended to include the nutritious and energy giving food along with you.

It takes a little knowledge and a planning sense to pack your bags with most appropriate items, while going for a hunt. And you will praise yourself for your smart planning while enjoying the adventurous sport.

Elk Hunting: An Art

Elk are really royal animals and it is really a major challenge for skilled hunters to hunt them. You are fortunate enough if you get a chance to see an elk a large sized animal during your career of hunting. You will surely admire elk for its big size.

The elk is a shrewd animal like a fox and it is also a rare and vague creature. There are many hunters who have never got a chance to see hulk and many have made unsuccessful attempt to shoot elk.

The process of hunting elk is very slow and it requires a lot of patience. It is not possible to hunt elk without patience. If as a hunter you like to hunt many animals rapidly without much effort then you can't hunt elk.

You have to do a research on the manners of male and female elks for hunting elks successfully. Autumn is the hunt season for elk and also the mating season for elk and you can imitate many activities and manner to attract the animal.

Some activities are required to be done during specific time of day. Certain degree of temperature can put great effect on behavior of elk. You can do one more important research for elk hunt and that is the research about the food and water resources of elk.

There are many options for hunting elk like many other hunting activities. Rifle hunting is very common activity. There are some other hunters also who like muzzleloaders and bow hunting.

These processes of hunting have other problems related to them. These methods require great proficiency and marksmanship. Hunters those come under this category are people who like to do challenging tasks.

Each kind of hunting process consumes its own time and it has its own limitations. You must be aware of the local hunting where you plan to hunt. The gun suppliers also tailor their goods for these kinds of hunting processes.

They provide hunters or muzzleloaders during their visit. In this way the gun suppliers fulfill the basic requirements of hunters for elk hunting.

The economy of many states has enhanced as they have provided areas to hunters for elk hunting. These states have seen the come back of hunters and outsider fans by using good methods for conservation of elks every year.

All this has boosted local economies and even private hunting areas. Some hunters visit for a chance to win trophy elk and on the other hand some come for just enjoyment of hunting in good areas. Some rich hunters just come for fulfilling their fancy of hunting elk. Hunters get the experience of hunting for which they have cherished.

Elk Hunting: Heed The Call

Elk are very big in size and this is the reason why elk hunting is considering very special kind of hunting by hunters.

These large sized animals have different type of life style and the mating customs of these animals are also different. These animals can be deliberately violent or coward.

The hunters who participate in elk hunting activity regularly get very less chances to come near this royal creature. They can tell very less stories regarding their experience with these large creatures. The weight of a male elk can easily reach to eight hundred pounds. The elk are very shrewd and it is really a complex task to kill elk. The hunting of elk requires a great skill on part of hunter.

The success of elk hunting practice depends on many elements. Time is the major element for hunting elk. An experienced elk hunter can easily understand that how much time is required for elk hunting.

They can also tell about effect of temperature on elk hunting.   Those who wish to hunt an elk for first time require hiring the services of a guide. Elk can be found in many areas. A guide can help in making a successful attempt of elk hunting by offering value able tips to the hunter. Thus can guide can be very helpful for you for elk hunting.

Bugling or announcing is the second important element for elk hunting. This is the activity, which is performed by the male elk for challenging other males and for attracting females during the mating season. Hunter also does this practice but it can be dangerous if it is used excessively.

The effective use of this type of practice is possible only if hunters have vast experience to have information about the places for use of this method. In this way an experienced hunter can use this technique more effectively.

You can find many manuals and books in the market, which can give information regarding use of bugling while hunting.

You can also find calls, which can imitate female elk or cows. Some hunters make use of these devices to attract a bull closer during hunting. After sending the bull at a beneficial place one can make a move for final attempt. You can make a successful shot after attracting the bull.

The excessive use of bugling can prevent the male elk from coming near to advantageous area during hunting. The good quality of instrument ensures the good quality of results. Elk have inherent quality to foresee dangers.

You can hunt an Elk only by creating a natural environment. Thus it is necessary to make the elk hunting practice more and more realistic.

Elk Hunting: Rifles

The use of black powder cartridge rifles for elk hunting practice is a famous skill of refutable elk hunter. This is preferred option of those hunters who like to perform hunting practice life their ancestors. They would like to use age-old method of hunting.

Some hunters consider it misty and murky method of hunting. This method is considered to be very suitable and well organized method for different kind of hunting games.

It requires a great skill and time for making a successful attempt of elk hunting with help of black powder cartridge rifles. The people who select this method of hunting have to spend a lot of time for doing practice.

There will be a greater contentment after every step of enhancement and success.

Those hunters have many options to consider who choose to hunt elk with black powder. You have to learn many things to get access in the practice of elk hunting.

One has to take a decision regarding caliber, butt stock, length of rifle, sights and selection of material along with selection of type of rifle

One also has to learn the method hand load ammunition. This is a very tough task to learn but with practice one can easily gain proficiency in it. It is common thing to hear about hunters that they have to cast their own bullets.

Hunters not only have to devote time for practice but also have to spend time in field for learning effective handling of firearm when they wish to learn elk hunting with powder cartridge rifles. This type of practice of elk hunting needs important amendment and it is very different from modern method of elk hunting.

Elk are very obscure creatures and enormous creatures and they also have thick veil and big internal organs.

Everybody is aware of fact that the firearm and ammunition that is used for elk hunting must be very strong to handle the task of elk hunting successfully. This is necessary when there is no option for automatic reloading in this type of elk hunting.

One more facet of elk hunting with black powder is that of cleaning. The large amount of powder can make things untidy for the hunters. Regular care and cleanliness of weapon is essential for keeping it fit for hunting.

The gunpowder can settle at several parts of gun and can make it hard. The efficiency of gun can be spoiled due to collection of gunpowder at many places. The shooter should use blow tube for preventing the powder from hardening until the process of cleaning of gun is over. You can find many kits for cleaning black powder cartridge guns

Elk Hunting: In Arizona

The experience of Arizona elk hunting is same for a keen elk hunter as the experience of F1 GrandPrix race for a racing crazy motorist.

This type of hunting is considered to be best big game hunting practice. The hunters get chance for this type of hunting during fall season. During this period the hunters go for Arizona elk hunting in the hope of getting a trophy bull. The inspiration for hunting the most obscure creature of animal world is really a challenging task for hunters.

The Rocky Mountain Elk is very ordinary type of elk, which is found on an Arizona elk-hunting trip. This kind of elk is also referred as Wapiti. The weight of male Rocky Mountain Elk is 700 pounds or even more than this.

The internal organs of rocky mountain elk are covered by a ribcage, which includes a very hard cartilage, and it has a thick veil over its body. You require possessing right ammunition for making a direct shot and the shot should be effective and moral. In this way it is real challenge for a skilled hunter.

Arizona elk hunting season starts in the fall months of mid-September through October also. During this period elk go for their mating season. Elk males get angry, start bugling loudly and start searching for females for mating.

The most important facet of elk hunting the use of elk calls by hunters. It is essential to have knowledge about these calls.

There are certain types of calls, which let the hunters, to imitate bull or cow elks. You must be aware of the time and method of use of calls for luring the elks. The less and excessive use of bugling may prevent the elk from coming near.

They will run away from such an area where they foresee any danger. In this way you will miss the chance. You can hire the services of a guide for a successful move of hunting elk in Arizona.

This step will be really beneficial for you if you are not aware of the geographical condition of Arizona and you have very less experience about this practice elk hunting.

You need the help of a guide even if have experience about Arizona elk hunting. A good and expert guide can help you in hunting an obscure elk and can also offer you helpful and valuable tips regarding this. The outfitter can also help you in dragging the large creature once you shoot it.

You cannot even imagine doing all this all alone. In this you should surely hire the services of an outfitter to hunt an elk in Arizona and this will beneficial for you.

Elk Hunting: How To Succeed

If you have knowledge about bow hunting and you wish to check your efficiency in hunting then you would like to do archery elk hunting.

The main reason behind this is that the elk is the biggest game animal for hunting and it is also a very cunning creature. This is really a challenging task that every hunter would enjoy to do. It is a biggest accomplishment in itself to hunt an elk with the help of bows and arrows.

Bow hunting is a subtle and complex sport in itself. The use of bow is more difficult if you are already into archery elks hunting.

An archery elk hunter should be able to make an exact estimation within given time that will be required for taking out and leaving a bow and he or she should be able to understand the game properly.

There are many things which one has to keep in mind to gain success in process of archery elk hunting. The things which one is required to keep in mind are:

1. You require a special kind of bow, which is structured to kill a large animal life elk. This kind of bow is remarkable piece of device. The bow hunter has to gain information about every facet and capacity of his hunting equipments.

The length of arrows, which are used in hunting, should be proper. The arrows should be sharp enough to cut the thick veil and cartilage to make a clean kill. You need to do a lot of practice for killing an elk that possess several pounds of weight.

2. You must acquire every type of information. You should devote some time in gaining information about location of food and water resources for elk in that area.

Observe their behavior and manner during certain time period of day and also about the temperature. Just read the ideas in local wildlife reports.

3. Do the practice of shooting in heavy coats.

4. If you have to hunt elk from a tree then you should spend time in changing your establishments to gain proper viewpoint about location. All this has to be done before the hunting process.

Archery elk hunting is a complex process. . Fortunately there are many hunting tips of hunters who wish to do archery elk hunting. You can hire services of outfitters for getting elk hunting tips.

The guidance of an outfitter can prove beneficial for you even if you are an experienced hunter. Archery elk hunting can be really very satisfactory sport for a hunter who wins a trophy through it.

You will gain awesome experience even if you don't win trophy in elk hunting sport.

Elk Hunting: Using GPS

Perhaps you must have heard that a GPS - Global Positioning System - unit can assist you in the pursuit of deer and elk hunting. This technology has been made available by the U.S. Department of Defense for military pursuits; the technology is extremely affordable also.

Their method of working is very simple and remarkably complicated. The unit relieves a signal off the many satellites ranging the earth and –bingo- area is found.

The method with which they report the information keeps on changing but most commonly they recognize latitude and longitude.

A GPS division can easily become an important part of your hunting gear. It can help you in estimating the walking distance, search your way to hunting grounds with total accuracy, assess the time it will take for you to arrive at a destination, take account of fresh deer or elk.

In this way you can come back to them again. Most of the hunters who make use of GPS divisions   to map the area where they hunt for elk or dear.

When you go out for hunting you can keep the important items in landscape such as pieces of rock, bends in trials, creeks etc. You can these articles to make map on paper or computer.

You can spot the places on your map where you have seen marks of elk or deer. You can compare these sights with the surrounding area, you can easily get an idea of place where you can find dear or elk.

GPS units can provide you real help during you hunting activity. You can also make use of your GPS to help you in explaining where you are if you get lost. If you have spotted a waypoint on your GPS and design it as a truck or camp then you GPS may lead you back to home.

You can do the same function in case you have killed a deer or elk and unable to drag it yourself. You can mark the location as a waypoint, go back to meet some friends, and you can easily find a way back to your prey.

GPS can also be used for searching a way. If you shoot a deer or elk at any place then you can easily find a place where you have to take the prey.

It is not a necessity to use GPS but it is a great device to help you in elk hunting second time. You should always keep a pack of fresh alkaline batteries, as you never know when your GPS will run out of fuel. In this way GPS device can guide you in great way for hunting dear or elk.

Elk Hunting: On Private Ranches

If you want to learn the art of hunting elk, you must make arrangements for carrying out the procedure of elk hunting on the private ranches. The two significant places where you will find the availability of these ranches include the regions of U.S. and Canada.

These ranches are the most preferred places, as they provide a number of facilities like lodging facilities, good quality food and also, the expert guides. The most desirable feature of these hunting sites is that there is surety of getting the elk.

The rooms available for the accommodation of the guests are big and full of facilities like personal kitchens to cook and also, the hot tubs for bath. Moreover, you are also provided with meals while on the ranch for hunting.

The experience of hunting on these ranches is out of the world. There are a number of expert guides that assist you in finding the target. There are usually two hunters accompanied by one professional guide.

The authorities also provide the transportation facility to help you in the hunting. These transportation facilities include four-wheelers, ATV and horse rides.

The best part of hunting on these ranches is that it has a wide variety of these animals that include antelope, mule deer amongst the top species. Thus, you have the high probability of finding the elk with ease for hunting.

The kind of natural terrain of these ranches is the ideal place for hunting elk. There are some special features like rolling hills, forests with the web of oak trees along with the large number of pine trees and aspen trees.

The land that surrounds these ranches is full of wild terrain and thus, helps the hunter to easily put pressure upon the target animals.

Reasonable Rates Offered

Talking about the fees for hunting elk on these ranches, it is really wonderful to know that these ranches provide a number of facilities like lodging and meals at an unbeatable price.

There is no competition in the prices and the services offered by these ranches. The people who own these ranches have great flair for this adventurous sport.

The guides employed for helping the hunters also share the spirit of hunting with the hunters. Moreover, this hunting activity also provides assistance to the local owners in managing the crowds of animals.

The overall package that includes rooms for staying, three meals, expert guides and transportation facilities costs around $1500 that is quite reasonable.

The information about these ranches is available on Internet and travel magazines. Moreover, a local traveling company may also assist in finding the privately owned ranches for elk hunting. The ranches are indeed the great places for great sport.

Elk Hunting: In Colorado

Colorado is the place that holds the record of providing natural habitat to the highest number of elk population.

This large population of elk makes Colorado as one of the most admired places for elk hunting. The place has been successful in attracting a number of hunters every year to enjoy the adventurous sport.

The nature has provided Colorado with beautiful scenes that have led to the existence of a number of hunting grounds. These hunting sites are either publicly open for all, or are privately owned by the rich residents of the region. However, these private owners also provide the facilities for the hunters to experience the elk hunting in a better way.

The natural terrain is of different nature at different places. If there are green fields at some places, you may find forest areas at other locations. Yet, you can also find huge mountains in some areas.

Whatever may be the terrain, there is high probability of finding the elf, especially the female elk, which is hunted for the motive of food.

The hunters are provided with many services and thus, they have to carry very little stuff of their own that includes bedroll, clothes and food material. You can avail the services of experienced guides, who are there to assist you in hunting.

These guides also provide the accommodation to the hunters. It is recommended to book these services in advance to avoid rush. You may also be provided with information before hand about the things to be carried along with you.

Support For The Economical Development

This is just not an adventurous sport, but it also supports the economy of Colorado. Thus, the government has taken steps to conserve the species of elk in the region.

These efforts have shown some significant results, as there is an increase in the number of elks having good health.

The Colorado elk hunting has much more to offer to the hunters from various countries. It is not only a wonderful trip, but it also provides the chance to catch the wonderful landscapes of the region. And above all, you have the chance to hunt the animals from one of the most admired species.

The services offered are very easy on your pocket, as are offered at very little rate. Moreover, you may reduce the price of the overall package by avoiding the services of an experiences guide, however, it is advised to take the services of a guide.

There is provision of one guide for every two hunting groups. The guides are recommended for the hunters, who are the first time visitors to these beautiful hunting grounds. The other prices included are that of the license for hunting and also, other basic requirements.

Elk Hunting: The Best Time

Many people might be unaware on the big influence that time plays on elks. If you wish to hunt the elks, you need to appreciate what meaning the season has on the elks which will make you realize the reason why the elks behave in a particular fashion.

It will give you a clear idea as well, regarding what you need to do and what situations you will confront while you go elk-hunting. Being strongly influenced by the seasons of the year, elks go up a mountain or trail down. In the fall early on, being in the ruts, elk-hunting is a good option for hunters.

In fact at this season, you will experience many sounds known as 'bugling' which are made by the elks for the purpose of females and territory contest. Known as the 'rutting season' as far as elks are concerned, the bulls got separated from cows months ago, and they now begin stuffing themselves with fodder.

They have got back their antlers, and while they still retain their winter velvet, it sheds in summer as days reduce and nights lengthen. The antlers darken as rut forms upon them. The antlers are commonly mud-stained when you may see them.

A seasoned hunter should know about the disposition of the bull during this time. At summer, bulls wander mainly at mountains, having commonly males in them who are juvenile. They start losing their cool as days shorten with the passage of season.

Here the bulls gather near the cows to maintain seraglios which the bulls keep in bulk. Also, at this season, the humps as well as the necks of the bulls start swelling to almost double their normal size.

Besides, their hair becomes longer too, and coarser as well. So during rut, a bull looks much bigger than it actually is. Being high-tempered, you will need to approach them with caution at this time. But as soon as this season concludes, they will be back to normal. They will become very much calm as they normally are, and they will lose weight and be just as they were.

So this season's reactions in the bulls are to be taken care of by a hunter a big deal.

So after having read this article, it will be clear that keeping in mind the season of hunting the elks is very important indeed as they will make you appreciate their behavior and make you prepare for such kind of a behavior well in advance.

Elk Hunting: Using Black Powder Rifles

Some extraordinary sportsmen who love challenges go back to the traditional black powder rifles for hunting purposes. Having a limit of just a single shot, it poses a challenge to the hunters' expertise.

You will need to analyze the weather, and he must be fully into the hunt, and also be required to get pretty close to it. Being a weapon that is archaic, it gives the hunter a feeling of pride and satisfaction, and makes them feel close to their ancestors who used similar weapons for their hunting purposes.

More number of accessories is required to be carried while using a black powder rifle as compared to a modern one.

The hunter using black powder rifles requires carrying balls, powder, cleaning jags, ramrod, patches, solvent, a worm which pulls the ball and also a patch lube. It will test your skills of organizing though you may possess a bag big enough to accommodate these items.

Even otherwise, it tests your skills of judging the wind as the scent and the powder could easily be spread and be smelled by the hunt thus requiring you to be extremely cautious.

It is interesting to note that the reason why it requires the hunter using a black powder rifle to get close to the hunt is due to the limitations of the eyesight, and not because of a defect in such a weapon.

A modern weapon for hunting can help you view something located many yards away but this is not the case when it comes to a black powder rifle.

Actually, some hunters prefer to have a scope attached to their weapon, but traditionalists believe that doing so takes away the charm associated with black powder hunting.

Patience and accuracy – these are the key in case of black powder hunting since the hunter just gets a single chance to hunt. If he misses the target, the chance is lost.

Also, such hunting is of a completely different type, to which many hunters are not accustomed to. With a rifle that permits many shots, a hunter is assured that if he misses the target, he has a few more chances to hunt it down but such is not the case here. In case of black powder hunting, the hunter has to time his shot to perfection.

Even if the deer is right ahead of the hunter, he can't shoot unless he is ready with that perfect shot.

To sum up, black powder hunting requires total expertise in all aspects of hunting, like judging the wind, timing the shot, getting close to the hunt, being patient, getting the perfect shot, etc. When all these factors provide the desired result, there is no bigger accomplishment in the world!

Elk Hunting: Choosing The Right Gun

If you happen to experience the fun associated with hunting an elk or a deer, you must first and foremost choose the suitable weapon for the task. Some factors that are to be considered while selecting it includes the weapon weight, range of shooting and your comfort level with the weapon.

You must not take this decision in haste. Rather, you must carefully analyze the many rifles that are on display. It is of a paramount importance that the weapon suits you well; it being of a shorter or a longer length can be a source of difficulty.

Actually, the length of a rifle can be adjusted by a gunsmith to suit your purpose. Yet another aspect worth consideration is "drop", which is nothing but the distance between the stock and the cheek of yours.

While aiming, make sure that your eyes are able to clearly see the target. If this is not okay, then it can actually hit the cheek of yours on firing.

Weight is also a considerable factor for this purpose as you will be needed to carry the weapon every time. Ideally, the weight of a rifle lies between six to nine pounds. Lighter rifles, contrary to the general perception, are not a better option, though it cannot be denied that being light in weight, carrying them becomes easier.

But as far as accuracy goes, the heavier ones provide better focus any day. Also, they are able to shoot at long distances, their recoil being much less than those of their lighter counterparts.

Rifles aren't permitted in a few spots of hunting. A slug or a shotgun will be helpful in such a case. A shotgun (which is similar to a rifle) with exclusive sights besides a rifle barrel can be opted for. With this, the range of the shotgun increases. The 12 and 20 gauge shotguns are used pretty frequently, though the latter is better for hunting purposes.

However, if you want to rely on the traditional hunting method using a bow, then the selection of a standard bow becomes important. A compound bow is preferred over a simple one, since they are heavier and incorporate pulleys and cams as well.

The normal weight of bows is thirty-five to forty-five pounds, though they differ between states. You can also opt for the cross bow for hunting purposes, though it is not so frequently used.

It is thus clear that a good gun or a bow is important for hunting. A weapon shop will be able to clarify your further queries if you have any.

Elk Hunting: How To Bag An Elk

Need some hunting advice of elk from Colorado? You've hit the target! Colorado is a popular destination for huge population of elk in the US, and you surely can take tips for hunting of elks for fun or to satisfy your hunger. Given below are some expert tips.

To start with, Colorado abounds in hunting places for elks. These hunting places, at times, offer exquisite and beautiful scenery to capture your imagination. With all the rocky mountains and plains as the backdrop, you can have some great time hunting there.

Elks are normally found in the trains of the given terrains, no matter if you locate those in the woods, the fields, the huge mountains or any other place. So this necessitates hunting elks as relying on finding them is not a good idea.

While hunting elks in Colorado, decide whether you require a guide or you will be able to do it all by yourself. For an expert hunter, hiring a guide would certainly mean wastage of money. Otherwise, a guide can be of immense help.

For starters, the guides will provide you with a perfect hunting spot not requiring you to do the homework yourself. A guide is aware of the various hunting places for elks, so his services will help you save quite some time and efforts. If you prefer multiple hunters, there are group rates offered by such hunters.

Timing is very crucial for a master hunter. Hunting is required at all seasons. So if you miss out on a hunting chance once, it might as well end your hopes for another hunt in the season. Another aspect of timing is the hour of the day you go to hunt.

Temperature can be a factor of hunting as well. These are three among the many factors that you need to take care of prior to hunting for elks in Colorado. For this, a guide will be of help as he is accustomed to the many factors which surround the hunting experience in Colorado.

There is a certain device known as the electronic callers which can be of immense help. They make sounds of female elks, which attracts the male counterparts. If you utilize the device properly, a catch of an elk will surely be a big catch for you!

But elk hunting is an art. Excessive or subdued activity can send caution signals to the elks and they can prepare themselves for it. Like in case of electronic callers, a bad quality device will draw the male elks away because they will sense danger when the sound suddenly fizzles out. So keep these tips with you which will be of help during all times.

Elk Hunting: Elk Calls

Hunting elks is considered to be a special activity, mainly because hunters consider elks as a very good prey. Also, elks are huge animals and have big rituals of mating and calls.

Depending on the season, they may be extremely short tempered or even timid. All those people who are experienced in hunting elks or have heard about them from anyone must be aware of the strange behavior of elks at times.

A bull (basically a male elk) can weigh around 700-800 pounds. But still, elks are the seasoned hunters' favorite because it requires a lot of patience and perseverance to get near those unpredictable animals, and one needs a lot of skill to hunt them down.

There are many aspects regarding great hunting of elks.

Timing is one essential element. The mating season, which is the fall, is the best for elk-hunting. An experienced hunter is also aware of the time when there is a lot of activity of elks and also the time when they are static.

They are also aware of the effect the temperature can have on elks. For beginners, it is necessary that you have a learned guide who will help you out in various aspects. As the elks can be traced in wide areas, the guide can assure you of where the animal will be found, besides giving you valuable suggestions for hunting those elks.

Bugling is a wonderful element of hunting the elks. A male elk or a bull uses the bugling to meet females during the season meant for mating, and by this, he also imposes a challenge on other fellow bulls.

Using bugling sounds can be a great tip, but using it excessively or in a subdued manner can alert the elks. The hunter therefore must posses enough experience so as to realize as to where to draw the line. Generally, almost all the markets come with a distinctive feature about how to use the bugling sounds accurately and to perfection.

Apart from bugling, there are instruments that mimic the tunes of the cows (the female elks) as well. To attract a bull, this is used by many hunters. When the hunters find that the bull has come within a close proximity of him, he can prepare a good shot and hunt the bull down.

Even in this case, proper use is the key. Using excessive or very little of the sound can make the elk cautious, and you may not get your hunt.

Also, make sure that you are using the mimic instrument of a good quality, else it will fail for sure.

Elks are very famous for being cautious about impending danger and being on their guard, so it is recommended that the sound must be very realistic so as to misguide the elk.

Hunting: Plan The Perfect Hunting Trip

Introduction

Hunting is an increasingly popular pastime for the whole family. With growing numbers of women taking up the sport, the opportunity to create special memories with the whole family in the outdoors is better now than ever before. And whether you're an experienced hunter, have been on a couple of duck or deer hunts or are just getting started, there are plenty of questions that need answering along the way.

Most of these are questions you end up musing over for a long time and never bother asking anyone. After all, these folks have been here before and asking what the draw weight of a bow for hunting elk is will mark you out as an inexperienced dullard. But fear not – there are no stupid questions, and the best way to learn about hunting is to experience it. In the pages that follow, we'll aim to give you a useful outline of the information you need to get started on your first hunt or a dream adventure for big game.

The key to success in many areas of life is proper preparation. Hunting is an excellent example of this. Regardless of your experience level, being adequately prepared for the hunt will give you a distinct edge over other hunters in the area and can make all the difference between success and failure.

Of course, if you've planned your hunt to the nth degree, there's still every chance you won't bring home a kill. The most important thing to understand is that hunting is much more than running around the wilderness slaughtering animals. It's an experience – one that generations of hunters around the world have learned, taught and shared with their friends and family across time. And the benefits each individual takes away from that experience vary just as much as the people who hunt.

Choosing Game

There is plenty of wild life out there, as anyone who's ever set foot into the less built-up areas of the world knows. And across North America, you can bet that plenty of people are making plans to hunt at least one thing in their local area in the coming seasons. Commonly hunted animals include the deer and elk, while more exotic species like bear, prong horn and sheep are also hunted in some areas.

If four-legged prey isn't your style, there is plenty on offer in the skies as well. Many bird hunters make their start on ducks and then move on to larger wetland birds, like the goose or move to upland bird hunting in pursuit of pheasant, grouse or quail. Other bird hunters see ducks as the ultimate hunt experience and see little reason to diversify.

There are many keys to a successful hunt, and the first of these is choosing something you'll enjoy hunting. If you like camping and spending time in the mountains or woods, then deer, elk or even big game might be what's right for you. If you'd rather do hunting in a more limited timeframe, and like the water, then a duck or goose hunt is more likely to match your style and preference.

You'll need to consider your physical aptitude for pursuing some game – animals renown for living at higher elevations can present unique challenges for hunters who aren't in the best possible shape. That isn't to say you need to be superman to hunt, it's just important to consider all the variables when choosing your target.

What can be hunted, when you can hunt it, how you can hunt it and where you can hunt it are variables controlled by regional fish and wildlife departments. And even if you think you know what's allowed, the best option is to consult your local fish and wildlife department for an updated copy of the regulations in your area. The majority of states make the guidelines for hunting available online, which makes researching the regulations for game you're interested in hunting in any given area easy as pie.

Choosing The Right Weapons

Once you're familiar with the regulations and decide on the game pursuit that's right for you, you'll need to be sure you've got the right weapon. For some folks, this is simply a matter of checking the family gun cabinet to see what's lying around. For others, choosing a weapon is a completely new endeavor that must be carefully considered to get the best results.

First, you'll have to decide whether you're going to hunt with a gun or a bow. Some game is best hunted with a gun, hands down. But other game can be had with reasonable success using either weapon. It is important to consider whether a bow is right for you – it requires a different sort of fitness and determination than gun hunting.

If you've never used a bow, there are a number of training courses, books and DVDs available to help you learn the craft of bow hunting. Ultimately, many of the options for bow hunters come down to personal preferences developed over time. So, if you're just starting out look into clubs in the local area that offers a 'get to know the bow' type course that you can take. This will help you get familiar with the ins and outs of bow operation before you're faced with a shop counter or catalog packed with hundreds of bows that you've no idea how to evaluate. Once you're familiar with bow operation, choosing a new long, composite or recurve bow will be easy and you'll be able to readily determine which accessories you'll need to make the most of your bow during a hunt.

Similarly, you can take training in firing all manner of firearms through local gun clubs and other organizations. Whatever weapon you opt to hunt with, the important thing is that you must be able to use it accurately. Far better you go into the woods with an old .270 Winchester you've used thousands of times before and maintained religiously than with a new, state-of-the-art rifle you've only fired twice.

This isn't the last time we'll tell you that practice makes perfect, or as near to perfect as you can get in the hunting arena. Whatever your weapon, mastering it is another essential key to becoming a well-experienced hunter. Knowing your weapon is about practice – and not just on the range. You'll need to practice aiming and firing, of course. But a number of people overlook the importance of routine maintenance and practicing weapon repairs.

When you're in the field, if something goes wrong will you be able to fix your weapon or will your day be ruined? A number of veteran hunters recommend taking along a spare, or backup, weapon for those just in case moments – but being able to repair and maintain your chosen weapon is just as important.

One final point of consideration is taking the right weapon on the right hunt. This isn't about having the right brand of gun or the right logo on your arrow heads, it's about making sure you've brought the right tool to do the job. You wouldn't try to change a light bulb with a screwdriver – and by the same token, you shouldn't go hunting grouse with a .30-06 unless you're just interested in watching feathers fly up into the air and then delicately drifting back toward the earth. If that's the sort of display you were after, it'd be far simpler for you to stay at home and sink a few rounds into some old pillows.

Assuming you are hunting for something other than a bizarre form of personal amusement, you'll need to do a little research and decide what the best weapon for your hunt will be. Again, this is a point where asking fellow hunters through bulletin boards and community networks can prove invaluable.

Essential Hunting Supplies

There are a number of things you need to remember to bring along for any successful hunt. Sure, there are plenty of hard-core pack hunters out there who go alone into the woods for a week with nothing more than they can fit into a mid-sized pack frame. And yes, these guys get results. However, what they pack is essentially the same as what we're recommending you load up for your own hunting party – just an ultra-light, streamlined version.

First things first, pack your weapon. Pack the right ammo and bring an extra box. Also, bring your gun cleaning kit or bow maintenance bag so you can go to sleep at night knowing your weapon is ready to go at first light. As mentioned, if you can, bring along a spare weapon just in case. While you're at it, include a strap or sling that makes carrying the weapon easier. And, because you don't want to worry about your weapon or ammo going missing while you sleep or being involved in a hunt-related accident, bring along a suitable storage case for keeping the weapon in while you're sleeping. The days when hunters thought it was ok to just throw the guns in the back of the pickup are long gone – what's more, a number of areas and hunt organizers have regulations that prohibit this sort of behavior. It puts you and your hunt pals at risk, making it both irresponsible and dangerous.

In addition to the weapon, you'll want to bring something to help you see what you're hunting – a good pair of binoculars or a solid fog-free scope is highly recommended. If you can manage, bring both. When choosing a scope, consider the lens size and magnification power. A 4x40 scope, for example has a magnification power of four and an objective lens size of 40 – the larger the first number, the closer the object will appear to you, the larger the second, the brighter your image.

Look for a scope that offers an element of eye relief, meaning you can use it without holding it right up to your eye, to avoid self-inflicted eyestrain. Binoculars should be set up ready for use – this means practicing with them before you take them into the field. Similarly, you'll want to be sure to pack sunglasses and any prescription glasses you need, as well.

Get a map of the area if you haven't got one already. You can find all sorts of maps on the internet, but sometimes the traditional, accordion-fold variety are simply better for detail and ease of use. Studying a topographical map of the area can help you find little-known hidey holes and low-lying openings where games are more likely to hide during the high-pressure days of the early season. You can always cut the map down and laminate the two sections you're going to be using to refer to them in the field. Which brings us to another piece of indispensable gear - a good compass.

Today's gadget-oriented society might make you believe a GPS is all you need. And, in fairness to those folks, a reliable GPS is great. The thing you've got to consider, particularly when hunting in dense, mountainous or unfamiliar areas is: where will you be if the batteries are flat? No one knows. That is precisely why we recommend you still bring a compass and a map of some sort. The old technologies are often best.

Another key area some hunters overlook is what happens 'after the shot' – it is important to prepare for victory if you intend to succeed. This means bringing along the things you need to properly care for and field dress the game you claim while hunting. For birds, this amounts to a sharp knife, some meat bags and a cooler. For larger game, you'll need a pair of sharp hatchets, a small saw, a sharp knife, a sharpening stone and suitable bags for storing the meat.

You might want to consider bringing a hanging kit to help you in your effort to gut, quarter and otherwise prepare the animal for transport. There are brief details later in this guide of what you'll need to do with these tools – for more specific information, you'll want to consult your fellow hunters, read a book and ask your butcher for any preferences they have regarding the handling of your animal.

Preparing For Your Hunt

Hunters who go into the field with all they need for each phase of the hunt do better, it's as simple as that. Prepared hunters get better results, have fewer accidents, enjoy their time on the hunt more and are always keen to learn how they can perform better the next time. The old saying, prior planning prevents poor performance, is definitely true when it comes to the hunt – and we make no apologies for reminding you that being prepared is the key to success. So, prepare for your hunt in every conceivable way.

First, know the habits of the game you're hunting. If you're hunting quail for the first time, talk to people who've hunted it before. Ask them for tips, and more importantly, evaluate the advice you're given against your own research – some people like to talk the talk, but that doesn't mean they can walk the walk. It's important to know that the advice you're given checks out in the field.

Don't be shy about checking out books from the library, making enquiries with online game hunting forums or pitting the opinions of your friends and family against one another – the results could surprise everyone, and a little information goes a long way when it comes to planning a successful hunting adventure.

The next key to planning a successful hunt is knowing the terrain you'll be hunting in. This takes two forms – first, understanding the type of ground you're likely to encounter, and second, physically scouting the territory you're going to be hunting. Researching the habits of the animal you're going to hunt will give you a fair indicator of how the animal behaves, what sort of cover it hides in, where it likes to eat and sleep. You can take that information and apply it to the actual ground you're going to cover.

Visit your hunting ground and get a feel for the likely areas you'll find the animal in question. Seek out areas where you'll be able to watch for animals, as well as areas you'll be able to hide in and take that perfect shot. If you're unable to visit the area in person, ask people who live nearby what their experience of the land is – granted, they're unlikely to reveal their favorite duck blind, but they might be able to give you pointers that will help make your trip more fruitful.

Pack well – don't overlook the standard items you should include and don't leave things out in the name of saving space. Truth be told, you don't know what you'll rely on most until you're in the field and by then, if it's something you've left at home, you're simply out of luck. Make a survival pack, which doesn't need to be any larger than a fanny pack, and keep it with you always. This should include a space blanket, a bottle of aspirin, a few nutrition bars, two eight-ounce juice cartons and a packet of water purifying tablets.

In addition to this, be sure you take a properly-stocked first aid kit. Refer to the basic Red Cross guide for what should be in a first aid kit and you can't go too far wrong. Bear in mind you need enough first aid supplies to tend to more than one wounded person – accidents happen, and so do stupid things. You need to be prepared for both, so stick a mini first aid kit in your vehicle, a full-sized one at base camp and another mini kit in your daypack in addition to your survival pack.

When you're packing for camp, include enough supplies for everyone in your party plus at least one spare of everything. Always bring more food and drink than you'll actually get through, in case you end up staying longer than you intended. Pack a box of waterproof matches into any nook or cranny you can find – matches are one thing you can't do without, and you never realize they're gone until it's too late.

Finally, the most important part of properly planning your hunt is letting people know where you're going. This should include: a rough schedule of when you intend to be where and when you will return; a map illustrating where you'll be hunting with any areas you know you'll explore highlighted; emergency contact numbers; and, details of who else is in your party. Leave a copy of your plan with a relative or close family friend, as well as a work colleague.

You should also post a copy of your plan in the appropriate area of the recreational park or forest that you're hunting. The point of this is to give search and rescue teams a fighting chance of finding you if there's an emergency or if you don't return home in due course. Making a proper hunt plan at the outset of your journey gives them a place to start – without it, they're charging blind into thousands of acres of woodland.

Hunting Well

Some beginning hunters opt to engage the services of a hunt operator – this limits the amount of planning and discovery you'd usually have to do on your own and offers a solid opportunity for you to get acquainted with a variety of the common aspects involved in successful hunting. These operators are available for groups or individuals, but prices can be high and it's important to go with a widely-renown operator to get the most of your experience.

Another tip for having a good hunt is making sure you go with like-minded hunters. If you're a beginner, it's ill-advised to go trekking into the brush without someone who has at least a little more experience than you. However, if you go hunting and haven't got anything in common with the rest of the party you'll be awfully bored during the down time. And depending on the weather, there could be a lot of down time.

There are a handful of unwritten rules for hunting, and it would serve you well to know them. For starters, always treat the weapons, wilderness and wildlife with respect. The majority of rules for a successful hunt are common sense things, such as: carry weapons pointed in the safest possible direction, never toward people; don't store firearms with chambered rounds overnight; don't sleep, climb a tree or jump down from a tree stand with a loaded weapon; only take a shot when you've got an unobstructed view of your target; and, don't drink alcohol while pursuing game, don't drink alcohol around loaded weapons and only consume limited alcoholic drinks following the day's hunting.

Another big thing that all hunters should remember is that a successful hunt isn't necessarily going to end with you bagging a trophy. Sure, that's the idea, and it's a great bonus if it happens – but a successful hunt will teach you something more about the game you enjoy pursuing, educate you about the terrain you've covered and hopefully improve your senses and other hunt-related abilities. Hunting is an opportunity for all of us to learn a little, teach a little and appreciate the natural wonder that surrounds us all year long.

And finally, you may've noticed, our greatest belief is that people get the most from their hunt experience if they're properly prepared for it. We're often told to hunt smart rather than hard – and that's solid advice. By preparing for all aspects of the hunting process, you're less likely to waste time covering terrain you needn't have bothered with or straining yourself physically due to inappropriate commitment. So prepare, pack and plan your socks off and when the big hunt comes your way, you'll be able to enjoy it.

Harvesting Your Hunt

If you intend to make a plush rug out of that gorgeous brown bear's hide, you'll need to be prepared in advance. The same goes for getting the most from that elk or caribou meat you're eyeing up – that's right, we said it before and we'll say it again: plan ahead.

When you're hunting for a big game trophy or the aforementioned bear skin rug, you'll want to consult a local taxidermist for specific instructions regarding handling your animal carcass. Though the principles for preserving the head and antlers of most four-legged species are relatively similar, each taxidermist has their own way of mounting a trophy – and if you fail to follow their specific instructions, you're unlikely to get the best possible result. So talk to a taxidermist, or if you intend on doing the mount yourself, read up on the best practice and take a brief how-to guide written on a 4x6 recipe card that you've either laminated or sealed in a small zip-top bag. Having the card to hand will ensure you're able to get the best of your catch in terms of display.

In brief, a head mount will need to be carefully removed, and this is best done by stringing the animal up so you can 'cape' the animal without worrying about blood or debris getting on the head. Think of how a cape falls across your own shoulders, and don't cut anything on the animal above the place that line would translate to them. This will make doing the rest of your field dressing tasks a bit more complicated, but overall the job of meat preservation takes priority for most hunters.

Now, to preserve your trophy, make an incision around the animal along this cape line. Then, work to carefully roll the hide forward from there, right up to the ears. You'll always want to leave more hide than is absolutely necessary for your taxidermist to work with – after all, it's easy to cut off any excess, but impossible to 'make' more hide if what's available falls short of requirements. Next, cut the neck about three inches below the junction of the head and neck. Once that cut is complete, you should be able to twist the head off by gripping the base of each antler firmly and applying a reasonable amount of pressure.

The other leading consideration for hunters is how to best preserve the meat they've won. Again, this is something with basics that remain the same across virtually all species we hunt. The most immediate concern is getting the meat cool, as this helps protect the meat from spoiling.

To field dress most birds and small game, all you'll really need is a good hunting knife. For larger game, you need significantly more than this. The essentials are a good hunting knife, a compact folding saw, a hatchet and a sharpening stone. You'll also want to take along some rope to stabilize the carcass while you're working and a kit to hang the animal if you need to.

Whether you're field dressing your kill for meat preservation or to create an exquisite trophy, a good tip is to bring a couple pairs of rubber gloves while you're working – they'll keep some of the grot off your hands, give you a truer grip on the slippery bits and, most importantly, provide a little protection against nicks and cuts.

Whether you opt to skin your kill, bone, quarter or simply haul the animal out whole, there are a few things you've got to consider. First, heat is the enemy. You need to cool that carcass down if you want to eat the meat at a later date, the fastest way to do this is to gut and skin the animal. The quick and simple guide to gutting is as follows:

- Slit the animal from anus to brisket (or lower, depending on your requirements) – take care not to puncture the innards

- Cut carefully around the anus and genitals, again taking care not to puncture anything

- Reach inside the upper-end of the cavity and work to roll the innards down and push them out the end of the animal. Cut away the diaphragm to gain access to the upper body cavity

- Continue cutting organs from the upper part of the body cavity out, carefully going along making precise cuts the whole way. The innards should slough out through the bottom of the carcass easily enough, bear in mind that if you intend to save the heart, kidneys or liver, you'll need to pack them in bags and get them on ice as soon as possible.

- Once the innards are removed, you may need to quarter your animal to pack it out

Second, once you've packed the animal away from the kill site and have it back at your base camp or in your rig, you need to find a way to keep it cool. Avoid storing the carcass in an enclosed space, like a car trunk. Third, you've got to keep the meat clean – that means free from debris as well as bugs.

One good tip for fending off insects is dusting your kill with a can of black pepper, and a solid piece of advice for keeping dirt at bay is to skin with great care so there's a layer of fat remaining around the carcass. Finally, secure your game properly for transport – the last thing you should do is tie it to the hood of your vehicle. Instead, be sure it's properly bound in the rear of your ride. On the other hand, you should be careful not to limit air flow around the meat – limiting air circulation can lead to spoilage and make the rest of your efforts all for naught.

Rewards Of The Hunt

Whether it's a stunning trophy buck mounted on the wall or a delicious meal made from meat harvested by your own hands, the rewards of hunting are many.

On average, a deer will yield around fifty pounds of meat. You'll convert just under half the weight of most commonly hunted game into meat if you wish to do so. You can opt to butcher the animal yourself or take it to a local butcher – there are advantages to handling the carcass either way, but most people will opt to take the easier road of using a butcher. Bear in mind that all butchers operate differently, what's common practice to one guy will be a completely unthinkable process to another. So, as with all other things, you'll need to be prepared.

If there's a local butcher you know and trust, use it. Otherwise, check with fellow hunters, friends and family in the area and see if you can come up with a couple of butchers to talk to. Once you've had a chance to discuss the butcher's working approach, you'll know which one is most suited to your own needs. Butchers will produce a variety of cuts of meat for you – so it's important to discuss your requirements both before the hunt and as you're handing the hard-won carcass over to the butcher afterward.

As part of your planning process, remember to ask the butcher for any recommendations you should follow when field dressing your kill as this will allow you to get the best results in terms of meat yield and quantity. Some butchers are able to fix your mistakes, in terms of how you've quartered the animal, for example. But, if your meat was too hot for too long and spoiled, was tainted by debris or some other substance, even the best butcher won't be able to do anything about it – and he shouldn't. At the end of the day, tainted meat will only make you ill, so there's no point arguing with the butcher about it. Of course, you can take the carcass to another butcher for a second opinion, but if the meat is spoilt, it's spoilt and there's nothing you can do but learn from your mistakes to avoid them in the future.

If you've been fortunate enough to get an animal worth mounting, you'll be gutted if you roll up to the taxidermist's shop and present something he tells you can't be mounted. So, as always, prepare yourself for success by visiting the taxidermist beforehand. Follow the instructions your taxidermist gives you in the field, pack the mount according to his guidelines and the odds of having a gorgeous memento of your best hunting experience are greatly improved.

One final tip for successful trophy mounting, be sure the wall you're going to hang the mount on is up to supporting it. The rack on an elk can weigh twenty pounds alone. Add to this the weight of the skull, stuffing, mounting board and accessories and you'll quickly be beyond the support rating of a mere nail in drywall. You'll also be out of the range for a normal picture hanger – so find a good stud wall and get the right sort of bracket to avoid having your trophy come crashing down.

Perhaps the most lasting reward of the hunt experience is one of the most often overlooked. Your memory. Of course, you and the other guys in your party will each have your own take on the whole experience, which will lead to amusing late-night arguments for years to come. But more than this, particularly if you've hunted with younger family members, you'll have a lasting image of something truly special. An experience that friends and family across generations come together to learn, teach and experience together.

The meat, if it isn't spoilt, will last a few months. The mount will stay on the wall until it goes out of fashion or is replaced by something bigger, better or rarer. But your memory of each hunt experience sticks with you until the lights go out. And that's something truly special.

A Bird Hunter's List

A few things should be on every bird hunter's list before he begins planning his hunting trip. Whether the hunter is looking for geese, ducks, turkeys, or quail, there are a few necessities to make every hunt a success. Some supplies will differ depending on the bird sought after, and many supplies cater to two types of birds, those that live on the ground, and those that fly. A hunter should know which supplies apply to the type of bird he's seeking.

A hunter wanting a challenge who's looking to shoot birds that fly will need a rifle with at least ten cartridges. There is no time for a hunter to pause between shots to load his gun. Also necessary will be a camouflage shirt, and a boat for goose or duck hunting. If hunting with a dog, a decoy will also be a handy tool. In a hunter's off time, the decoy makes a good tool to keep the dog well trained. There are also the basic supplies needed for every hunting trip; a tent, extra clothing, supplies for cooking, first aid, waterproof bags, and a mounting area for your game. The mounting area will be essential for keeping your prizes safe at night from other predators; a mount that is raised above the ground is often the best choice.

A few other supplies, depending upon the bird that is sought, may greatly increase a hunter's chances of success. Bird calls prove an essential tool in any hunting trip. Each call is specific to each bird, so if a hunter enjoys hunting many different species of birds, a different call will be necessary for each. A call, while sometimes expensive, is well worth the money when used properly. While most bird hunters hunt exclusively with guns now, hunting with a bow and arrows was once a popular way to hunt land birds. If a hunter wants to try his hand at this type of hunting, the local outfitter can advise the type and size of arrow to hunt with for each species of bird. There are also many instructional videos available for the hunter that is just starting out. These videos can be an invaluable resource, even to the experienced hunter. Also, for many duck hunters, a boat is essential. While shooting from land is an option, duck hunting from land doesn't often make for a successful hunt. While spending the money on a boat may be difficult, for the dedicated duck hunter, it is his most important piece of equipment. There is no better place to find ducks than on their turf.

The local outfitters store will have all the supplies listed above, with many more to choose from. The employee's at the store are often extremely knowledgeable about their products and can help with any questions a hunter may have.

Bow Hunting Equipment: Buying vs. Renting

While it may be tempting for the hunter to run out an buy everything he needs when he decides he's going to start bow hunting, this can be a costly mistake. The best option is usually to rent equipment. Many new bow hunters make the mistake of buying ill-fitting equipment, or just don't stick with the sport after a few hunts. The best option for the new bow hunter is renting so he can try out both the equipment, and his new found sport.

Renting equipment is the best option for the hunter because it allows him to get the experience he needs with a relatively low investment. Just because a hunter shows interest in a sport, doesn't mean it will become his new hobby for every spare weekend; there is much more to bow hunting than meets the eye. Bow hunting has long been considered a great challenge, which is why gun hunting has become much more popular over the years. It often takes years to master the shot that produces a clean kill every time. Bow hunting also requires the hunter to get much closer to his target, which is both an adrenaline rush, and a safety hazard. For the dedicated hunter, it is these challenges that keep him bow hunting through the years.

Many Pro Archery shops have an expert on hand to assist you in all your hunting needs. These professionals are often trained to best assist their customer, you. The best time to visit the local archery store is at a time of the day that isn't busy, mid-afternoon on weekdays and early morning or late evening on weekends. For a new hunter, one on one attention is what he needs. There are many questions to be asked and a professional that is rushed with other customers will ultimately leave you feeling cheated. A new bow hunter needs time to feel different bows and insure he finds the right fit for his frame. The professional will be able to gauge the right pull weight for the individual hunter, and in this case, stiffer isn't always better. The wrong fit can cause a hunter to not use the bow, or mangle his shot.

For these reasons renting bow hunting equipment is often a much better choice for the novice hunter. It will allow him the freedom to use top quality equipment, without sacrificing much money if he realizes that bow hunting isn't the sport for him.

A Bow Hunter's Shopping List

While most hunters use guns now, there was a time before the gun was around where all hunting was done with a bow and arrow. Hunting with a bow and arrow gives the hunter much more of a challenge, and much more skill is involved for a successful hunt. Hunting with a bow is also more retro; harkening back to the beginnings of man when hunting was necessary for survival. To start out bow hunting though, a few supplies are required, and doing some research can help a hunter determine what's right for him.

The biggest investment a hunter will make is on his bow and arrows. A bow should not be an item to go cheap on. Price is in direct proportion to quality in this instance. A cheap bow will result in poor kills, or no kills at all. Browse your local archery store and talk to the expert about what type of hunting you want to do and the best bow for the job, but don't buy just yet. Find a few favorites in the store, then go home and do your research. Doing the necessary research will result in an investment you'll be using years down the line.

Arrows are another item you should have in great supply. Always have extra on hand; wounding an animal and not having enough arrows to finish the job can get very ugly, very fast. Another supply to always have extra of is bow wire. It's not uncommon for the wire to break when pulling it back, not having extra on hand will make for a very disappointing trip.

Another item that is often overlooked by the newcomer is a leather glove. Pulling back on the bow can be much tougher on the hands than most people realize, having the glove to protect it will make all the difference between a good hunt and a bad one. Many hunters develop blisters and chafing because they didn't realize they needed gloves. The glove will also help to improve your grip on the bow, which in turn improves your shot.

Bow hunting is an adventure harkening back to ancient man. There is no better way for a hunter to feel in direct connection with nature than pulling the wire taut, aiming, and then releasing the arrow at the target. Be sure to wear gloves on every trip, and spend the time and money on a good bow and arrows to increase the chances of a worthwhile hunt.

The New Enthusiasts Guide To Bow Hunting

There are a lot of things to know before stepping into the field on your first bow hunting trip. A lot of people come to the sport knowing someone who can teach them the basic guidelines, but others must teach themselves. A lot of research will be necessary and there are some guidelines to know before even stepping into the store to buy your first bow.

Some people buy under the misconception that it is best to have the heaviest bow they can use. This is definitely not the case. It is essential for a bow to feel good in a hunter's hands; otherwise he won't get true shots, or won't use the bow at all due to discomfort. The only time it is good to use the heaviest bow possible is when hunting for big game, such as elk, ox, or bear. A strong bow can also be used in 3-D tournaments when using very fast arrows and a flat trajectory. Otherwise, when hunting whitetail, turkey, and even small black bear, using a compound bow in the 50 pound weight range is the best choice. This size can put an arrow all the way through the target, while still being comfortable for most hunters to handle. The only exception to this is when using recurve bows, in which they require a larger weight. Women usually prefer a bow in the 45 pound range.

The most important factor when choosing a bow is finding one that fits the individual hunter. Bows are not one size fits all, and different types and brands will all fit differently. Be sure that it is comfortable in your hands. It should feel balanced in your grip, and you should be able to pull the bow at its draw weight comfortably. Many hunters use bows that are too heavy for them; they assume that the bow will either loosen up, or that their muscles will develop more when using it. Using a bow that is too heavy can throw off your shot and ruin your accuracy. Another important thing to do when shopping for a bow is to browse around. A name brand bow isn't always the best choice for every hunter. Choosing a reputable brand with good construction is important but be sure to browse around too. Spend what you can afford, and buy the bow that is best for you.

The last suggestion for newcomers to bow hunting is to shop at an outfitter with an archery expert. An experienced hunter who knows his way around bows is often able to make a good decision, but a newcomer needs some guidance when making his first investment. The archery expert will be your number one resource in regards to buying your first bow.

A Short Hoof On Deer Hunting

Of all the types of hunting there is, deer hunting is one of the most popular. Deer are, for the most part, an abundant source throughout the United States. Because their behavior can vary depending on certain factors such as weather, time of day or even mating season, they are often considered to be quite an appropriate challenge for hunters. A hunter has to know how each factor working alone, together or in a combination will affect the hunt. With deer hunting, one can opt for the use of a rifle or bow and arrow. As long as one is adhering to rules and regulations of the season, hunting can occur on either private or public hunting grounds.

Deer are known to be nocturnal animals. Because they travel to and from feeding areas moments before sunrise and sunset, hunters are often given thirty minutes before dawn and after dusk to hunt. As with other animals, the moon will also have an affect of the movement of deer. When deer hunting, the seasoned hunter knows that a successful hunt often relies on planning accordingly. It is necessary to know not only what time the sun will rise and set but the moon cycles and how it will affect the day's activities. Those who tend to go deer hunting when it is only convenient for them often end up frustrated at their lack of results.

Even those who do not hunt know that deer are super sensitive animals and their innate sense of danger can have them moving at the tip of a hat. Aside from the need for food, the sound of wind, rain and even falling snow will put deer on the move. Despite camouflage and a number of other tricks, deer still tend to easily catch the scent of nearby hunters during hunting season. When deer hunting, the use of deer stands, a type of platform securely set in a tree, is often a first choice for hunters. This puts hunters up and over an area giving them a good view of the surrounding location they are hunting.

Many take to deer hunting during the fall mating season. It is during this time that deer behavior is most erratic and incautious. As many have found, this month long period is not only extremely active, it is not uncommon to see bucks and does out in the very middle of the day. During other times of the year, the middle of the day is a rest period for deer that have been out foraging all night long. The chance for a successful hunt increases during this time and it is not uncommon for hunters to take advantage of it.

Deer Hunting Basics

Deer hunting is without a doubt the most popular hunt practiced today. Deer are, generally speaking, a very abundant resource and can be found throughout nearly all of the 50 states. While they don't offer any kind of danger as say, overpopulation of bear, deer do a lot of damage to vegetation, particularly a farmer's crops, and they are by many considered to be a nuisance. Deer have very heightened senses, so while there are so many around, they aren't necessarily an easy target for the hunter. Deer behavior often depends on the weather, the time of day, and the time of year. A hunter must develop a sense of deer habits, and many, weeks before deer season even starts, will begin their bait piles and sit in their hunting blinds just to observe the particular deer coming to their area. The hunter has the choice to hunt deer with either a gun, or a bow and arrow, and providing the hunter knows the rules and regulations specific to his area, deer hunting can occur on either private or public land.

Deer can be a fairly elusive animal to catch site of. They are generally nocturnal, which means they do all of their wandering at night, starting to move around just before sunset. While hunters may not hunt at night, hunting regulations usually allow for this fact about deer and allow hunters to hunt for a short period of time both before sunrise and after sunset. Deer movement can also depend on the cycle of the moon; those who attempt to hunt only when it is convenient for them will often be disappointed.

Deer are highly sensitive animals. Any sense of danger and they're off and running at the drop of a hat. Even when no danger is present, such as a sudden shift in the wind, or snow or rain, can set deer moving. Despite camouflage, deer very often can sense a hunter's presence, most often by the smallest of movements a hunter may make to readjust, or because the wind is bringing the hunter's scent directly to the deer.

Many deer hunters use a tree stand when hunting. This is an elevated platform anchored securely in a tree and provides the hunter with a better view of the area around him. Deer hunting is generally done in the fall mating season when deer behavior is at its most erratic. During this one time of the year the deer are generally much more active, and will often come out in the middle of the day when they would normally be resting. The hunter, if possible, should use this to his best advantage for a successful hunt.

Helpful Deer Hunting Supplies

Hunting deer can be a game of waiting as opposed to hunting. The process of hunting deer requires a lot of patience because of how flighty the animal is. If they sense any type of movement, they'll run. They also are very hard to lure to certain areas. Since deer usually live in wide areas, this can pose a problem. Luckily, there are deer hunting supplies that can help keep you hidden and lure the deer to you. Buy these deer hunting supplies for your next trip into the woods.

One of the most popular deer hunting supplies is the deer stand. These are little stands that you fit up onto a high point of a tree trunk. From there you can play the waiting game. It may take more than a day for you to see any deer. Because of this, it is very important to have a tree stand. It will give you more of a chance that you won't scare the deer away. As an added bonus deer stands also give hunters a good vantage point of the area around them. You can see much farther from a deer stand. Because of this, you can shoot much farther as well. Always practice safety, though. Make sure to harness yourself onto the tree stand. Since you'll be up high on a little platform, it can be easy to fall off. There have actually been hunting accidents where people have fallen off of their deer stands and broken bones. Don't let this be you.

Another great addition to deer hunting supplies is the deer game call. Since deer are very hard to lure to an area, you should use all means at your disposal. Deer calls make sounds that sound just like a real deer. This will often lure deer into the area. Deer are a very social animal and they travel in packs. They may think that your deer call is the call of one of their deer friends. They will then come to the call. This is a great addition to the deer stand. While you're high up in your perch, you can use the call to lure the deer into the area. From there, you can shoot at will. Using both deer hunting supplies in unison will drastically raise your rate of success.

The next time you plan a trip to the woods to hunt some deer, don't forget to bring these valuable deer hunting supplies. They can help you bag some of the finest deer you would ever hope to hunt.

Deer Hunting Supplies

Deer hunting tends to be much more of a waiting game than a hunting one. For an impatient hunter, waiting an entire day or more without the slightest sign of a deer can be torture. Because deer are a highly sensitive animal, they are easily startled and at any sign of something unusual, whether it be sight, scent, or sound, they'll steer far clear of the area. Introducing some supplies to help your hunt can be a great way to get a peek at a deer much sooner.

One of the most popular deer hunting supplies, some hunters would say a necessity, is the tree stand. Having the bird's-eye view from a tree can give the hunter an entirely different perspective on his target. Being elevated also aids the hunter is remaining hidden from the deer; it is much more difficult for them to hear or pick up the scent of a hunter when he is more than a dozen feet off the ground. If you decide to use a tree stand though, be sure to be very cautious; many hunters have sustained serious injuries from falling out of their stands. Use a harness to ensure the utmost safety.

Deer often roam large territories, so having a deer wander into your line of site at the right time can be extremely difficult; another great addition to your deer hunting trip is a deer call. As with any call, these take a lot of practice to master, so don't expect to walk into the woods a master right out of the gate. The call can be a great tool in stepping up your game when used the right way. The call mimics the sound of a real deer, and since they are herd animals by nature, if there are deer in the area, your call should lure them in. Using both the call and your tree stand together, these tools can greatly increase your chances of a successful hunt.

As when investing in any hunting equipment, always do some research, both by talking to an expert at the local hunting store, and by doing some research online for product reviews. As in the case of choosing a tree stand, finding the product that is right for the kind of hunting you want to do will make all the difference between a successful hunt and a miserable one.

The Basic Deer Hunting Tips For Success

Most hunters are well aware of the techniques to employ when hunting deer, but newcomers and amateurs may need some deer hunting tips to get started down the right path in hopes of bagging that first buck. Here are some points to start with when hunting deer.

â€¢ Start early. You'll notice that the hunting seasons are limited by dates but also be daylight hours. No guns are to be fired before sunrise or after sunset for the safety of all hunters involved. However, one of the best deer hunting tips you can follow is to start early. You should be in your deer stand or hunting blind before sunrise. Getting there that early will diminish the possibility of being noticed by the deer and allow you to be in place when the first specimens begin coming out for a drink and a bite to eat as the sun rises.

â€¢ Stay late. Those who have gathered knowledge and give out deer hunting tips frequently will tell you that the best times to bag a deer are sunrise and sunset. The lighting at these times of the day can actually confuse the sight of the deer, and they will be out in greater numbers because, aside from filling their stomachs at these times as a rule, they will be less likely to see you.

â€¢ Avoid scents. Do not wear perfume, cologne, after shave, or even strongly scented deodorant. Keep unnatural smells to a minimum so that you disrupt the highly sensitive sense of smell that a deer has as little as possible. Human smells spook these animals easily, and one of the best deer hunting tips to keep in mind is to let the wilderness cover your smell. This is one of the few times in life you may be better off showering later rather than in the morning before entering the woods.

â€¢ Most of all, keep in mind that silence is the key. While you are out there to have fun with your friends, deer also have a keen sense of hearing and anything above a whisper (and even a whisper if it is a particularly quiet day) can be heard by many cautious deer. This is the most important tip among deer hunting tips, as even the slightest sound as you are lining up for a shot can lose that prized buck for you.

While there are more detailed tips available to make sure you get the most out of your trip, these deer hunting tips are the basics and will get you started down the road to success and enjoyment as a deer hunter.

Basic Deer Hunting Tips

While to some it may seem obvious the right things to do, and not do when deer hunting, for the newcomer there are some tips that may are well worth mentioning. Deer hunting isn't as simple as walking into the woods with a gun, there is a lot of preparation required, but following these few guidelines, a hunter will greatly increase his chances of bagging his first trophy.

• Start Early. Hunting season is limited to only a certain time of the year, and only at certain times of the day. Firearms are not to be discharged before sunrise, or after sunset. This protects the safety of other hunters in the area, because at these times there is not enough light to reflect off the hunter orange every hunter is required to wear. Some states however, allow guns to be fired one half hour before sunrise, and one half hour after sunset; check local regulations for further details. Keeping this in mind, a hunter should still use the law to his best advantage; head out to your blind well before sunrise. This will allow you to remain better hidden from any deer in the area, and when sunrise does come up and the deer are moving around, the hunter will be ready and waiting in his blind.

• Stay Late. While some hunters choose to hunt the entire day, sunrise and sunset are the best time to find the deer. Depending on local regulations, a hunter should start to head to his blind well before sunset, around mid-afternoon, and stay for as long as the law will allow, at most one half hour after sunset. If a hunter is only able to hunt a limited time of the day, these are the two best times to do it.

• No Scents. Before going out to hunt avoid any unnatural smells; this may be the one time of year when a shower may not be in a hunter's best interest. No perfume, cologne, or after shave, and beware of strongly scented deodorant. Deer have a very sensitive sense of smell, and even the slightest scent can alert them to a hunter's presence.

• Absolute Silence. While this may be a slight exaggeration, silence is essential when deer hunting. Very low whispers only, and if that can be avoided, all the better. Hunters often underestimate a deer's heightened senses, so be sure to stay as quiet as humanly possible, otherwise your trophy buck may be long gone before you even get a peek at him.

While there are a lot of other things to know to increase your chances when deer hunting, these are the basics a hunter should keep in mind before heading to the woods. Following these few rules will help a hunter bag the trophy he's been dreaming of.

Great Duck Hunting Dogs Are Worth Their Weight In Gold

Waterfowl hunting, also referred to as goose hunting and duck hunting, is an outdoor sporting activity enjoyed by people all over the world. Many hunters use duck hunting dogs to retrieve their downed ducks. Duck hunting dogs not only retrieve dead ducks from cold water and difficult terrain, where a hunter could possible be injured but duck hunting dogs also search for and recover wounded ducks. These wounded ducks could escape or die a slow, painful death. Because of their keen sense of smell, well-trained duck hunting dogs usually have no problem finding and retrieving ducks shot by the hunter.

Small game hunters using shotguns normally have gun dogs or duck hunting dogs, which primarily hunt waterfowl and small game. The three classes of gun dogs are pointing breeds, flushing spaniels, and retrievers, which are all good duck hunting dogs. They train pointers to locate their prey and stand motionless, pointing at the bird or small game. These duck hunting dogs point or freeze to keep from flushing the game until the hunter gets into position. Most pointing dogs will retrieve downed birds. Pointers are loyal, affectionate dogs that make wonderful pets and love to hunt. English pointers, German shorthair pointers, Irish setters, English setters and German wirehaired pointers are great duck hunting dogs.

Flushing spaniels or flushing dogs are duck hunting dogs that hunters have used for several hundred years. Hunters train them to stay close, usually within thirty-five or forty yards. Flushing spaniels work close, so the hunter gets great shots at the fast flying ducks the dog flushes out. English Springer spaniels are great flushing duck hunting dogs and make a great housedog. These dogs are loyal, compassionate, and extremely intelligent, with natural hunting abilities. English springer spaniel flushing duck hunting dogs work hard, are good tempered and love hunting.

Retrievers are duck hunting dogs that recover the ducks or other waterfowl without damage to the game, because of their soft mouths. They are quick to learn, easy to train, enjoy hunting, and love to please. A well-trained retriever can mark, follow hand signals, retrieve to hand and knows many more commands. The hunter commands his or her retriever to mark and the dog looks up for a falling bird. There are times when it is necessary for a retriever to follow hand signals. Hunters must be able to direct their dogs remotely, in some situations, so hand signals are extremely important. The retrieve to hand command is where a retriever puts the waterfowl directly into the hunter's hand. Great duck hunting dogs are worth their weight in gold to a hunter.

Different Breeds Of Bird Dog

Many duck hunters consider their bird dog an essential part of their hunt. Because of their loyalty and passion for the hunt, these dogs jump into cold water, or retrieve over rough terrain to get the bird their master has killed. A good bird dog is definitely worth his weight in gold to the serious bird hunter. If not for the dog, hunters would lose many a downed bird. A well-trained bird dog adds an entirely new dimension to the hunt.

There are three types of bird dog, all with a slightly different angle for hunting; the pointing breeds, the flushing breeds, and the retrievers. Pointers are very disciplined and able to locate and freeze when they find prey. They stand motionless, allowing the hunter to get into position and then they flush the bird. Pointers are also able to retrieve downed birds. They are loyal, affectionate, and make a great family pet. English pointers, German shorthair pointers, Irish setters, and German wirehaired pointers are all examples within this category.

Flushing dogs consist mainly of the spaniel breeds; the English springer spaniel is the best known in this category. These dogs have been used for hundreds of years and have been trained to stay close to the hunter, within 30-40 yards. The English springer makes a great housedog; he's intelligent, loyal, compassionate, with natural hunting abilities.

There are many different types of retrievers, the Labrador retriever being the most widely known. They excel at retrieving game because of their soft mouths. They've also become one of the most popular family pets because of their sweet temperament, trainability, and their eagerness to please. The retriever also stands out because of its ability to learn hand signals; a hunter motions for the dog to look up, and the dog is able to follow the bird's fall and know where to go to retrieve it. They are also extremely good at "retrieving to hand", meaning they put the bird directly into the hunter's hands upon retrieval.

When choosing a bird dog, a hunter's choice will lean heavily upon his own preference. While a dog should be eager to please and have a love for the hunt, the most important thing a hunter must have with the dog is a rapport. Oftentimes a hunter is simply just drawn to a certain dog, and as long as the dog exhibits all of the other basic traits, that's the right dog for him.

The New Duck Hunting Gear Available Makes Hunting More Comfortable And Enjoyable

Waterfowl including ducks populations may vary and a hunter's success often changes but duck hunting gear just keeps improving. These duck hunting gear improvements include ammunition, clothing, boats, motors, blinds, gun dog training methods, decoys, and other hunting equipment.

Many hunters believe that the modern, duck hunting shot shells and ammunition available today is far better than lead shot from years ago. Some of the major improvements include higher velocity loads and non-toxic shot. With this improved duck hunting gear, hunters can successfully shoot ducks from further away and have far more choices available in ammunition.

Camouflage hunting clothes are certainly improved duck hunting gear. There are duck hunting garments nowadays, made from extremely lightweight, waterproof materials that keep you comfortable and dry far longer. The new hunting jackets are wind proof, keep the hunter warm, are lightweight and give the duck hunter's freedom of movement.

They make duck boats much more advanced and specialized today than the boats from years ago. Duck boats are an important part of the necessary duck hunting gear used for navigating lakes, cattail sloughs, swamps, big rivers, and streams. Manufacturers of watercraft realized the importance of boats for waterfowl hunters and today, almost every major boat manufacturer got on the bandwagon and now produces waterfowl/duck boats. There are Jon boats for duck hunters that come in many different lengths, models, a big selection of camouflage paint colors, and have accessories available such as a built in fuel tank, grab rails, gun storage boxes, lights, bilge pumps, center or side console steering, ice chests, and bench seats. Some duck hunting boats even have lockable dry storage and shelving for storing decoys, shotguns, and many other duck hunting gear items.

Both land and boat duck blinds today have undergone huge transformations with better designs, materials, and superior construction. When it comes to duck hunting gear, the new duck blinds are easy to install, portable, compact, affordable, lightweight, and hide hunters efficiently. The boat blinds are made of rugged nylon fabric, with sturdy frames, and easy to setup, attach, and take down.

Duck boat motors have also undergone a variety of important changes over the years. Surface drive model mud motors move both larger and small duck boats across water-related obstacles such as logs, sand, mud, swamps, weeds, and other things that would bog down or destroy the old water-cooled, conventional outboard engines from years ago. Compared to years ago, today's modern duck hunting gear certainly makes hunting easier and far safer for duck and waterfowl hunters. Hunters are now comfortable while they enjoy their favorite outdoor activity.

Improvements In Duck Hunting Gear

Duck hunting has come a long way over the last decades. Hunting years ago used to be an uncomfortable undertaking that only the passionate partook in, but with all the new advancements, duck hunting is more enjoyable than ever. Improvements have been made in the way of ammunition, clothing, boats and blinds, motors, and decoys to name just a few.

Many modern hunters will attest to the fact that ammunition has come a long way since the days of old. Years ago lead shot was used which was toxic to everyone who came into contact with it. Ammunition today has higher velocity loads and non-toxic shot, which means not only can hunters be safer, but they can also shoot from farther distances.

Clothing is another item that has made great strides since days past. The modern hunter now has lightweight, waterproof, warm, camouflaged clothing to choose from. Being comfortable while out in the field is the number one thing a hunter can do to improve his changes of success; having breathable clothing that a hunter can move in is absolutely essential.

Duck boats have probably made some of the best improvements when it comes to duck hunting. The hunter has many options to choose from, and picking the right one will depend solely on his preference and hunting style. Boats are now better able to navigate lakes, cattail sloughs, swamps, rivers, and streams more than some boats of the past ever could. Boat manufacturers have since recognized the importance of quality duck boats and now nearly any boat manufacturer also produces a hunting boat. Jon boats are often the most popular choice and come in a variety of different lengths, models, and camouflaged colors for the hunter to choose from. There are also many new accessories available, such as a built in fuel tank, grab rails, gun storage boxes, lights, bilge pumps, center or side console steering, ice chests, and bench seats. Some boats even have a locked storage box or shelving for decoys, guns, and other supplies. Along with the boat, the motors have also improved; they are now better able to navigate through obstacles such as logs, sand, mud, swamps, and weeds.

Both land and boat blinds have also seen a major transformation. Material is now made extremely lightweight and durable, and is made for ease of transportation. These new duck blinds are now easier to assemble and deconstruct and allow the hunter to have utmost comfort while he's out in the field. With all the new improvements catering to the duck hunter, he can now spend more time than ever engaging in his favorite pastime.

Duck Hunting Supplies Are Important For The Safety And Comfort Of Duck Hunters

Duck hunting is an outdoor sport enjoyed by men and women across the globe and duck hunting supplies are an important part of this sport. Most waterfowl including ducks are migratory birds spending their summers breeding up north in Michigan, North Dakota, Canada, and other northern locations and in late fall, most birds migrate south spending the winter in Texas, Arkansas, Mexico, Louisiana, South America etc. Duck hunters love the thrill of the hunt and prepare months in advance for the opening day of duck hunting. They drag out their duck hunting supplies and make sure all their equipment is in good shape. Some duck hunters keep it very simply using just the basic duck hunting supplies and tools such as duck decoys, duck calls, camouflage clothing, and a shotgun. The duck hunting supplies of other hunters sometimes includes a duck hunting boat and trained hunting dogs.

One of the most important duck hunting supplies is the duck gun. In Canada and the United States, the most common duck guns are usually semi-automatic shotguns or pump action shotguns although some duck hunters do prefer break action hunting guns such as over-under and side-by-side guns. Many western European countries, Canada, United States, France, and the United Kingdom banned toxic shot such as lead and now use steel shot, which is a cheaper but less effective alternative. Because lead is denser than steel, the range for steel shot, which is lighter in weight, is not as long. Duck hunters must get closer to the ducks in order to kill them.

One of the most important duck hunting supplies is definitely camouflage duck hunting clothing. During duck hunting season, which is usually in the fall and winter months, the weather can be extremely cold and harsh. For duck hunters, their clothing needs to be lightweight, warm and well insulated, waterproof, and allow them to move freely. Most duck hunters are in a boat, hunt over water, hide in a duck blind, or even stand in water. Duck hunting waterproof clothing is crucial for both the safety and comfort of a hunter, so be sure they are part of your duck hunting supplies. Waders, which are waterproof pants with attached boots, are necessary for any hunter standing in shallow or deeper water. Warm, well-insulated, camouflaged clothing is also necessary, as duck hunting, depending on your location, is often a very cold, wet sport. Duck have extremely good vision so without camouflage clothing; the ducks will definitely see you. Quality duck hunting clothing is definitely an important part of any hunters duck hunting supplies.

A Duck Hunter's Supplies

Duck hunting is a popular sport enjoyed by outdoorsmen from around the globe. Ducks are a migratory species, meaning they spend their summers in the northern locations, such as Michigan, North Dakota, and Canada, then when cooler temperatures hit, they begin a long journey south to warmer areas like Texas, Arkansas, Mexico, and South America. Many hunters prepare for months for the upcoming duck season and take great enjoyment out of every aspect of their sport. Especially when dealing with firearms, it's important to check all of your equipment to be sure it is in great working condition before opening day. Some basic supplies a duck hunter may have are: decoys, duck calls, camouflage clothing, and a shotgun. Some avid hunters may even spend time and money on a duck boat or bird dogs.

The most common gun for use in duck hunting in the United States and Canada is a semi-automatic shotgun or pump action, although some hunters prefer a break action gun such as an over-under or side-by-side. Most western countries, such as Canada, the United States, France, and the United Kingdom have banned the use of toxic shot such as lead. For safety reasons this is good, but the steel replacement poses more of a challenge to the hunter. Steel shot is cheaper, but less effective as it doesn't have the range that the heavier lead shot did; this means that a hunter must get closer to his target.

One of the most important duck hunting supplies is clothing. Most hunters prefer the use of camouflage as duck's have phenomenal eye sight, but check local regulations as hunter orange may be required. Duck's prefer wetland habitats, so the duck hunter often encounters wet situations while out in the field. Also, since duck season is done in the cooler temperatures of fall and winter, having appropriate clothing for conditions is essential. A hunter will get years of use out of his waders, a pair of waterproof pants with boots attached. This will allow him to focus on his target and not his steps to avoid puddles; he will also be better able to retrieve his kill if he's not using a dog. Finding clothing that is lightweight, yet very warm and well insulated will be the most important thing a hunter can do for himself. The hunter should be able to move well in the clothing, and waterproof wear will always be an asset. All too often a hunter underestimates the cold conditions and has to cut his hunt short due to inappropriate clothing.

Heeding The Call Of Elk Hunting

Elk are considered to be one of the largest of quarries for a hunter, making elk hunting a special type of activity. These large animals also have larger than life calls and mating rituals. They can be blatantly aggressive or relatively timid. Those who participate in hunting elk on a regular basis are likely to have quite a story or two of coming in close contact with these majestic creatures. A male elk, or bull, can reach seven to eight hundred pounds easily. Regardless of size, many hunters enjoy the challenge of hunting elk because they are extremely cunning and it takes great skill to get close to them.

Successful elk hunting relies on several elements. One of those elements is timing. Many elk hunters plan their hunt in the fall during mating season. The seasoned hunter also understands what time of the day elk are most active and when they are not. They also know how temperatures can affect a hunt. Those who are just beginning their interest in elk hunting would do well to hire a guide their first few times out. Elk can be found in a range of areas. Not only will a guide know the area well, he or she will be able to better ensure a successful hunt with valuable tips and advice.

Another element of successful elk hunting is called bugling. Bugling is something the male elk does during mating season to locate females and challenge other males. Hunters who bugle for males find it is the one delicate aspect of a hunt that can have disastrous effects when used either too much or too little. The effective use of this kind of call requires the hunter to have enough experience to know where the boundaries of using such an instrument are. Most calls on the market often come with manuals or recordings that demonstrate how to properly and effectively use the instrument.

There are also calls that mimic female elk, or cows. Many hunters also use these instruments during elk hunting to lure a bull closer. Upon getting the bull into an advantageous spot, one can move in for the final shot. However, as with the male elk call, vocalizing too much or too little can cause elk to stop calling or move out of an area altogether. When using such an instrument, many hunters find the better the quality, the better the results. Elk are well known for their ability to instantly discern danger in an area; therefore, it is necessary to sound as realistic as possible.

The Art Of Bugling

Elk hunting has long been considered an extremely challenging hunt. Elk are very sensitive animals and are weary of anything new or unnatural to their area; for this reason it takes a lot of skill for a hunter to track and get close enough to shoot. Another reason elk hunting is considered such a challenge is because they are known for being very unpredictable. Sometimes they are timid, and other times they can be very aggressive. It's important for a hunter to take great caution as a bull elk can easily reach eight hundred pounds.

It just so happens that the time of year most elk hunters prefer to hunt is in the fall mating season, when an elk is most active, and most unpredictable. This is especially the case for bulls, whose hormones are running in overdrive. This excess amount of testosterone in their system can cause them to be highly aggressive. It's important for a hunter to do a lot of research and know his quarry thoroughly. Studying elk behavior can be very helpful on the hunt, and especially for the first time hunter, hiring a guide to take you on your first few elk hunts can prove an invaluable resource. The experienced guides spend their lives tracking and studying elk, a hunter can do nothing better to increase his chances of bagging a trophy than hiring one.

Bugling is something a hunter will hear about profusely when doing his elk research. For many avid elk hunters, practicing their bugling becomes their hobby in the off-season; there is no such thing as too much practice in this art. Bugling is meant to mimic the call of a mate, so not using the call properly can have just the opposite effect and steer an elk far clear of the sound. As mentioned, elk are highly sensitive and cautious; if anything sounds amiss they will not allow curiosity to get the best of them to investigate. Bugling for elk really is an art form; a hunter must bugle enough to be realistic to other elk, yet not too much to make them weary. A hunter strives to perfect his craft in order to have the innate sense when enough is enough. That being said, don't be afraid to buy your first call and start practicing. Many come with an instruction booklet or audio instruction to demonstrate the proper sound. This can be a great resource for the hunter unfamiliar with bugling.

Looking For Good Hunting Dogs

How does one choose good hunting dogs without getting stung? Many dog breeders are like horse traders' you get what you get, and that isn't what was listed. So a dog breeder's reputation, letters of reputation or phone calls, and looking at siblings or mother and father of the dog means a lot when looking for good hunting dogs. Make sure they have some form of guarantee and for how long they guarantee the puppy or dog.

But what is good for one hunter may not mean the same for another, so make sure you know what you want before going out and looking. Do you want versatile good hunting dogs for all-purpose hunting, or one that is excellent at squirrel hunting or coon hunting? Look at where they will be living the remaining time' will it he be a family member? Make sure the breed you want is one you have information on and have done your homework on. Just because grandpa had one doesn't mean you know what you need to know regarding the purchase of good hunting dogs.

Good hunting dogs need to be disease from and have clean genetic lines, regardless the breed. Make sure routine worming has been done as a puppy' which has usually been done from two weeks. Also, look at their shot records' did they receive a two-week puppy shot series with only two weeks between them, beginning around five or six weeks? Once the puppy is weaned from its mother, its immune system becomes compromised, and it is up to the breeder to maintain that system up to eight weeks of age when it leaves the next. A breeder who sells before then is not worth his/her weight in salt. Good hunting dogs mean that' a good hunting dog, not one that is haphazardly bred to make a quick buck. Georgia is famous for good hunting dogs, as most Georgia hunters think more of their dogs than anywhere else, but make sure you don't get a bad breeder anyway.

Different breeds have different health risks' with the popular German Short

Finding A Good Hunting Dog

As many hunters can tell you, a good hunting dog can be worth its weight in gold. They become an indispensable resource to any hunt, and greatly enhance the hunting experience. Finding the best hunting dog for you can take a lot of time and patience, but when found, the hunter will find him well worth the effort.

There are some things to start you off on your hunting dog search. The number one thing a hunter can do is to always buy from a breeder. While there may be many postings at the local outfitters of hunting puppies available for sale, a hunter just doesn't know what he's getting. A breeder's entire business is based on quality and the hunter's happiness. Be sure that the breeder you go through is accredited by the state they practice in; if they are an open and honest breeder, they will be happy to give you this information and often show you their breeding certificate.

After narrowing down your choice of dogs at the breeder the second thing to be concerned with is the dog's health. Puppies especially are very susceptible to health risks if they haven't been taken care of properly. You want to get details about your dog's vaccination records. Any breeder worth his money will have very detailed records about each dog's shots and any health problems it may have had. The perspective buyer will want to pay special attention to the immunization records of the puppy's first few weeks. There are two times in a dog's life when it is most susceptible, when it is first born, and when it is weaned from its mother; at both of these times the puppy should have received shots to boost its immune system.

One of the last things to consider when choosing your hunting dog is its lineage. Most breeders take great pride on their detailed records, and talking to the breeder about your potential dog's parents and grandparents will give the hunter a great chance to see what his dog is made of. Make sure that they were all good hunting dogs. These dogs should not have been bred haphazardly to make a quick buck, two dogs are often chosen for their specific traits to be bred; talk to the breeder about what the characteristics are. If the breeder still has the parents or grandparents, even better. Check these dogs out to get a feel for your dog's genes. When choosing your perfect hunting dog, a hunter can never be too careful or ask too many questions. A quality breeder will welcome all of them.

Important Hunting Dog Medical Supplies

When out in the wilderness, you need to be ready for any type of situation. After all, you will generally be out in the middle of nowhere. That's why hunters normally bring medical supplies and first aid kits with them. Unfortunately, they tend to forget about their hunting dogs in that respect. Hunting dogs can get hurt, too, and they need just as many medical supplies as you. Because of this, you should stock up on some hunting dog medical supplies for your next hunting trip.

Hunting dog medical supplies are a bit different than humans' first aid kits. Dogs rarely benefit from emergency aspirin or from adhesive bandages. Instead, most of what's in a hunting dog medical kit is for serious injuries only. After all, most dogs are tough enough to handle minor injuries. One of the first hunting dog medical supplies you should get is gauze. There are occasions where a dog might get a flesh wound. This can happen if they get in a fight with another animal, or if they get caught in some brambles. You should carry gauze with you just in case this happens. When the dog gets hurt, clean the wound with some water and wrap it with gauze. They should be fine until the end of your hunting trip.

Another entry into your hunting dog medical supplies kit is a splint. Dogs are used to running around in tough conditions without thinking about their safety. This can cause some dogs to fall off of high places. If this happens, they may end up breaking a leg. This happens more often than you would expect. In a case like this, you should splint up your dog's leg with gauze and splint to keep in safe until you leave. If something like this happens, you should probably leave immediately. Broken bones are serious business and the leg should be looked at by a veterinarian. Because of the importance of this kind of injury, a splint is one of the must have hunting dog medical supplies that you should carry with you when you go on your hunting trip.

There are other, less important items that should be in the dog health kit. Most large pet stores carry a small kit that you can bring with you while you're in the wilderness. It will have all of the small items that you'll need, including tweezers and antiseptic ointment. Be sure to carry all of these hunting dog medical supplies with you during your hunt just in case of any emergency.

Hunting Dog Medical Supplies

While many hunters realize that first aid is important to carry in the field, many neglect the fact that their four-legged hunting companion also may need some medical attention. Dogs are tough and often with their adrenaline pumping can get into bad situations. When running at full speed through trees they can get cut and bruised easily, and a hunter has to be prepared for the different types of injuries their hunting dog can sustain.

A dog's first aid kit will be a bit different from the human variety; dogs won't often need emergency aspirin or adhesive bandages. While dogs are tough animals and a lot of the injuries they sustain will be minor enough to not need veterinary attention until the end of the day, there are some essentials a hunter should never be without.

The first thing a hunter needs to have in his canine first aid kit is gauze. Most of the injuries sustained by a dog in the field will be flesh wounds from the dog getting physical with another animal, or running at high speeds through trees and brambles. A hunter needs to not only carry gauze, but know how to use it. Tighter isn't always better, especially in the case of wounds near the feet. It's extremely easy for the circulation to be cut off in this area and the dog's foot can swell, so while it should be secure, don't wrap too tightly. Before wrapping the wound be sure to rinse it out with clean water; this wrapping will often be okay to last through the end of the day's hunting trip.

Another essential item to the canine first aid kit is a splint. Because of the adrenaline rush a dog feels when in the middle of a hunt, they often can get into careless situations, such as twisting or breaking a leg in deep holes or by falling from high places. This happens much more often than a hunter might expect and he needs to be prepared in case it does. The dog's leg will need to be splinted and wrapped with gauze. This injury is serious enough that the hunting trip should be cut short and the dog should be taken to a veterinarian.

There are other smaller items that a hunter should have for his hunting dog, and many animal supply stores carry canine first aid kits with just these types of items, such as tweezers and antiseptic. Be sure that you carry all of your canine medical supplies on every hunting trip in case a medical emergency should arise.

The Pursuit Of Hunting Elk

Hunting elk is known to be one of the biggest challenges in the world of hunting. Not until they have had a chance to come upon this majestic creature in person do many hunters realize just how massive elk can be. Even fewer realize the wapiti's ability for being elusive, until a puzzled hunter realizes all too late that their quarry has given them the slip for the second and third time. The elk's ultra sensitive nature allows it to detect danger almost immediately. This is what makes hunting elk the ultimate challenge. The hunter who prefers bagging their quarry with little or no effort is not likely to enjoy hunting elk.

When it comes to hunting elk, nothing guarantees greater success than studying the behavior of both the male and female population. During fall, when the hunt is on and elk are into their mating season, or rut, certain behaviors are carried out that, when mimicked, can either lure or scare off the trophy bull a hunter has been waiting to bag. There are some behaviors that are only carried out during certain times of day. Even certain temperatures can have an effect on elk behavior. Aside from learning where principal food and water sources for elk are located, learning these differences can be one of the most crucial elements for a successful hunt.

There are several different methods for hunting elk. While rifle hunting is common, there are those who prefer muzzleloaders and bow hunting. Each of these hunting methods presents their own challenge for those that use them, requiring various levels of skill and marksmanship. Hunters in this category are those that prefer extra challenge when hunting elk. Each method of hunting is given its own time period during the elk hunting season and has its own requirements and restrictions. Many outfitters also tailor their hunting trips for these types of hunting methods, providing services muzzleloaders or bow hunters might need during their trip.

Providing areas where hunting elk is a welcome activity has proven to be a great boost to many a state's economy. By applying effective conservation methods that ensure plentiful herds year after year, a number of states see a return of hunters and outdoor enthusiasts each season. This in turn stimulates local economies, especially in areas surrounding public and even private hunting grounds. While some hunters come for the opportunity to bag a trophy elk, others come for the mere challenge of the hunt in a beautiful setting. Either way, hunters are likely to have just the experience they have been dreaming of.

A Hunter's Greatest Challenge: Elk Hunting

Elk hunting has long been thought of as one of the most challenging trophies a hunter can seek. Because of their highly sensitive and cautious nature, elk can often sense danger well before the hunter realizes there's even an elk in the area. The elk hunt requires great skill and patience on the part of the hunter; he often must hike several miles off of the beaten path, be extremely quiet, and if he prefers to bugle the elk in, he'll need to be patient and practice the art of bugling with just the right finesse to draw the elk in and not scare them away. With all of these things in mind, one might wonder why it's worth the effort at all. For the hunter who prefers an easy kill, it probably won't be worth his time, but for the hunter who likes a challenge, there's nothing like breathing the cool morning air while waiting for your quarry to step into view.

A hunter must study elk behavior extensively before stepping out into the field on opening day. It's imperative to be familiar with elk behavior; where they feed, bed down, and spend their days grazing. Elk habits depend on many things, including the time of day, the temperatures, and the time of year. While it's important to know all of these things, much of what will be learned will often go out the window during elk season. This is because the preferred time to hunt elk is in the fall, during mating season, or what's also known as the rut. Elk, especially bulls, are often vastly different from their normal selves; with high levels of testosterone pumping through their bodies, they are often unpredictable and aggressive. They are also not as concerned with danger and the senses are dulled, which is why hunters prefer this time of year.

There are many different methods a hunter can choose from to hunt his elk. Rifle hunting is the most common, but some also prefer muzzleloaders, or even bow and arrows. Each of the methods will take great time and practice to master before getting a shot off at your trophy. The perfect shot often only comes once a season, so a hunter must have complete confidence that it'll bring the creature down. Hunter's also often prefer to enlist the help of a guide. The guide will be a great asset to any elk hunting trip, and many times they will tailor the adventure to the type of weapon the hunter will be using. Guide services also offer a variety of amenities to the hunter. Some provide the whole nine yards, from licenses, to lodging and food. Others provide only the guide; in this case the service can often give recommendations for places to stay in the area. The elk hunter greatly boosts a location's economy, and many small towns have come to depend on the influx of hunters each year. Many hunters return year after year to the same area because of the wonderful level of hospitality, and because the elk hunt is an experience unlike any other.

The Enjoyment Of Pheasant Hunting

Natives of the Asian continent, pheasants were brought to Europe in the tenth century and quickly became a favored hunting prey. The late 1880s saw the introduction of the pheasant into the United States from Great Britain, and they proved to be a great fit in their new habitat. By the 1920s, the pheasant population was high enough to allow for pheasant hunting which soon became so popular that there was a continuing demand for pheasants to be raised and released. As a result of agricultural practices in the 1960s, which created thousands of acres of prime habitat, that decade saw the zenith of pheasant hunting. Subsequent changes in farm policies brought about declines in habitat acres and with the decline of pheasant populations, the sport of pheasant hunting declined as well.

Skills necessary for pheasant hunting include, as with other prey, patience but silence is especially important. Pheasants are particularly sensitive to sound and sight, and it is very important to be as quiet as possible. Practicing the skill of walking and moving quietly will pay off in pheasant hunting success. Shooting skill is also vital, as pheasants are known for being extremely fast and agile enough to execute acrobatic movements in the air making them difficult to bring down. Having a well-trained bird dog to chase down wounded birds is invaluable for retrieving birds that are able to run. Even a bird that has been hit can still run long distances very quickly and elude the hunter.

Successful pheasant hunting requires a knowledge of the kinds of habitat pheasants prefer and why. Areas at the intersections of food and cover habitat or "edges" are an excellent place to look for pheasants as the birds spend a lot of time there. Patches of cover off the beaten-path should not be passed by, even if it takes a little longer to get to them. Later in the season when other more accessible areas have been hunted, the out-of-the-way places can still contain significant numbers of birds.

Consistently successful pheasant hunting requires the ability and willingness to seek out new habitat to hunt. Variations in weather conditions from year to year, changes in farming patterns, the number of other hunters in the area, as well as other factors, can change the pheasant numbers in a particular area from one hunting season to the next. Keeping informed of weather conditions, extreme weather events, and the projected number of pheasants expected to be in the area can be a guide to where the hunting is likely to be best and be a deciding factor in choosing an area to visit. Information about conditions in an area can be obtained from wildlife officials, friends, acquaintances living there, or even employees of sporting goods or hunting supply stores in nearby towns, thereby helping to ensure a successful pheasant hunting trip.

The Joy Of Pheasant Hunting

The pheasant has been a popular bird for hunting for many hundreds of years throughout the world. The bird is native to Asia and was brought to Europe in the tenth century where it quickly become the fowl of choice to hunt. It wasn't until the late 19th century that the pheasant was introduced to the United States from Great Britain. In the new habitat the bird flourished and by the 1920's their population was high enough that it became a popular species for hunting. Due to agricultural practices in the 1960's the pheasant population soared, then sunk in subsequent decades due to a decline in quality agricultural practices. Because of the declining population, the sport of pheasant hunting also declined.

Because pheasant have such a heightened sense of danger, they can be a very difficult quarry to track. A hunter must be very patient, and as silent as he can manage. It's necessary that a hunter take his time walking through the field when he's searching for a bird. Excellent aim will also be important as a hunter often only gets a few seconds at his perfect shot. Pheasant are known for the quick and agile movements, so bringing one down can test a hunter's skill. Using a well-trained dog can be an invaluable resource to the hunt, both in the flushing of birds and the retrieval.

For any species, a hunter must know the creature he seeks. Studying up on pheasant habitat and behavior will only prove to increase a hunter's chances and enjoyment while in the field. A hunter must have keen eyesight and always pay attention to areas that have both food and water available for the pheasant; they prefer not to travel far from these necessities. Another great place they prefer to hide is along deep ditches and the undergrowth of bushes and trees.

A hunter should also pay attention to the weather when he's hunting pheasant. Variations in climate and weather conditions can effect the pheasant population from season to season and thus effect a hunter's choice of hunting location. Another great resource can be online forums where hunters discuss local pheasant populations in the area. Here a hunter can find good locations to hunt, and patterns that other hunter's have noticed while hunting the fowl. Pheasant hunting can be a fun, and very challenging target for even the veteran hunter, so doing a little research will certainly put the game in the hunter's favor.

Texas Deer Hunting Rules To Abide By

In Texas, deer hunting is a favored sport and a way of life for many, especially when concerned with whitetail deer. While mule deer are also available, whitetail are plentiful throughout the south and especially in Texas, and hunters merely need to be aware of various regulations that will affect their ability to participate in Texas deer hunting.

First of all, Texas deer hunting regulations do not allow any type of fully automatic weapons. Rimfire ammunition, regardless of the caliber, is also forbidden. While hunting season opening and closing dates vary minimally based on the region of the state, regulations upheld during open season are the same throughout. All open hunting dates require that no firearms be discharged prior to half an hour before sunrise or after the close of the day at half an hour past sunset. Such Texas deer hunting regulations are set to protect hunters from friendly fire in lighting that is insufficient for recognition. Also, hunters in motion on the ground must have a certain amount of orange designation that will not camouflage into the environment. Check state regulations for exact requirements.

There are various Texas deer hunting areas that are considered public, but in order to hunt in these locations, a permit must be held. Also, there are many public areas in which hunting is not allowed. For example, no hunting is allowed in state or federal parks or refuges, or in wildlife sanctuaries, on public roads, or propagation or nesting areas. Some counties also have restrictions regarding firearm possession and discharge, so you will need to be aware which counties do not allow hunting (some even prevent the use of a crossbow or bow and arrow, especially in state-owned areas).

When harvesting deer, Texas deer hunting regulations do not require that you log mule deer, and you do not have to log whitetails taken with special permits (MLD permits, etc). However, in the wild, you must log every whitetail deer upon completing the kill on the reverse side of the hunting license for reporting purposes. Any kills not logged can result in fines up to $500 apiece.

Be sure to check size regulations set forth by any county for Texas deer hunting. Some areas require that the harvest measure a certain size between antlers in order to take a buck or, at best, in order to be considered a trophy.

In regards to Texas deer hunting seasons, they vary depending on deer type and region, but for the most part, the season will run from mid November to the early part or middle of December, with a few special circumstances stretching beyond in both directions.

Texas Deer Hunting Rules

Texas has long been known for its great deer population. Whether whitetail or mule deer, many hunters flock to the state to bag a trophy. There are however, various regulations that the hunter must abide by to ensure a fun and lawful hunt.

Texas deer hunting regulation prohibits the use of any fully automatic weapon, as is the use of rimfire ammunition. Regardless of the location, Texas law prohibits any firearm discharge outside of one half hour before sunrise to one half hour past sunset. This law is put in place to protect the hunter solely; with the limited amount of light it is too difficult to distinguish other hunters in the woods. Also, Texas requires that a hunter must wear a specified amount of hunter orange while hunting; check local regulations for specifics.

While Texas has thousands of acres of public land available for the hunter to hunt, it is required that he have a Texas license to hunt them. There are certain areas that may however not be hunted, such as federal or state parks, refuges, or wildlife sanctuaries. Hunters may also not hunt on public roads or in propagation or nesting areas. Some areas also have special stipulations regarding the discharge of firearms or the use of bows; check local regulations for more details.

While Texas does not require the hunter to log his mule deer or whitetail when using a special permit such as a MLD, they do require it be logged on the back of all other permits. Failing to report can result in up to a $500 fine per kill. Also be sure to check local regulations regarding harvest rules; some areas require a minimum size in order for a buck to be harvested.

In general, the Texas deer season runs between mid November through the early or middle part of December; check local rules for specific dates for the area you'll be hunting. While there are any number of areas the hunter may choose to hunt, doing an online search is often the best way to find land that may interest him. There are also many hunting leases available from Texas landowners that the hunter may choose to take advantage of. In the case of any hunting trip, it's imperative that the hunter use extreme caution while in the woods, especially while hunting deer in Texas; it is the most popular hunting season, so there are often many hunters in the woods.

With these few rules in mind, and dong research, a hunter can head out into the woods confident that he'll have a safe and happy hunt.

Ways Of Training Bird Hunting Dog

There are several ways that you can own your own hunting dog. The most popular way to do this is to go to a qualified breeder. These breeders will usually have already trained their dogs to become great bird hunters. If you get a dog from a breeder, you don't usually need to worry about getting any further training for the dog. Getting dogs from breeders isn't the only way to get a hunting dog, though. If you find a dog that you like from a kennel or for sale by the owner of the dog, it won't normally be trained at hunting or any other type of helpful service. If this is the case, you may have to get the dog trained before using it while hunting for birds. There are many ways for training bird hunting dog. Each way fits a different kind of person and different price range.

Training bird hunting dog isn't easy. That's why most people choose to have professionals do the job. There are two different kinds of professionals that are good at training bird hunting dog; ones that specialize in hunting and ones that do general obedience training. Most people prefer to have a trainer who teaches their dog specific bird hunting traits. This is the best move because they are learning things that are immediately beneficial to your hunting. The downside to this is that specialized trainers such as this are much more expensive than regular dog trainers. They see how much hunters want their services, so they raise their prices. If you can't afford this, you can always get your dog trained by a general dog trainer. These people aren't adept at training bird hunting dog, but instead are great at getting your dog to obey you in general. This is good because a well trained dog will usually be able to handle hunting with you. Although they don't have specific experience in hunting, they are still much better off then they were.

The cheapest method of training bird hunting dog is to do it yourself. This can actually be a free way to do it by getting information from the internet and using books from the library to help you train your dog. If you have your dog trained by a stranger, they will be less likely to follow your own commands and instead will be trained to follow the trainer's commands. If you teach the dog yourself, it will always be used to following its master's commands. Do research before choosing which method you choose to train your dog; whether it's with a specialist, general trainer, or by yourself.

Training Your Bird Dog

While there are several ways for a hunter to find a hunting dog, the best way is to go through a qualified breeder. This way the hunter will know what he's getting, and if getting an adult dog, it will often already be trained for bird hunting. If this isn't the case though, the hunter still has some options for getting his bird dog trained and ready to hunt.

Finding a quality bird dog can be a tricky thing. When answering an advertisement that has bird dogs for sale, a hunter just doesn't know what he's getting. Regardless of the way he gets the dog though, an important factor when selecting is getting a look at the dog in action, or seeing it's parents hunt.

Because training a bird dog can be a difficult task, many hunters choose to hire a professional. While this may be a more expensive option, the hunter can trust the quality of training the dog will receive. There are two types of training a hunter can choose from. The more expensive route is to have the professional train the dog in hunting techniques. While it's more expensive, it will also allow the hunter to get right into the field with the dog. The other option is to have the professional simply train the dog on obedience; having a dog that listens while hunting is the number one necessity in the field. Having a dog trained for obedience is also a less expensive option.

For the hunter on a budget, the last choice is for him to train the dog himself. This will take a lot of time and a lot of patience, but it certainly can be done. There is one solid benefit to this method too; the dog will listen to your commands. Sometimes dogs will only respond to their trainer, so if their trainer isn't the hunter, it can be a problem. There are also many videos available that guide the hunter in training his bird dog. The internet and books can also be a great resource when training.

Whichever method the hunter chooses to train his dog, there is sure to be one that is right for him. Be sure if hiring a trainer to do your research and check their references. With a little time the hunter will have a great time in the field with his new four-legged hunting companion.

Times Change, Turkey Hunting Basics Stay The Same

One of the most popular quarries for hunters is the wild turkey. Turkey hunting takes place in both the spring and the fall. This gives a nice opportunity for hunters that miss out on one season to make it up with the other. During the spring when turkeys have their mating season, many hunters go out at the break of day and use calls to lure out male gobblers. As many hunters know, no two hunts will ever be the same. While some hunts end almost as soon as they begin, others can make a hunter why he or she ever took up turkey hunting in the first place.

Scouting for turkeys is the first step for planning the successful hunt. Finding these habitats locally can be as easy as asking a neighbor or in some cases, whoever is working the counter of the hunting department in a sporting goods store. Those well versed in turkey hunting will venture out at dawn to areas where turkey have been seen and listen for gobbling. It is perfectly fine to use a turkey call so long as, upon getting a response from a gobbler, one does not respond in kind. It does not take much for turkeys to become wary and stop gobbling or move out of an area altogether. Too much gobbling in a single area can have quite a negative effect.

Because there are two turkey seasons, hunters are often urged to somewhat change turkey hunting tactics between the spring and fall. In the early season, males are looking to mate with as many females as possible, making them more than willing to investigate a hunter's calls. In the late season when much of the mating has already occurred, things can be a little more difficult but not impossible. Instead of mating calls, many hunters change their calling technique to concur with a turkey's gobbling style. Aggressive calls should be answered with aggressive calls, while soft calls should be answered correspondingly.

Another tactic to make things easier is to hunt in teams. An extra person can be key to a successful hunt. For example, when a hunter sets ups a certain number of yards behind a partner, he or she can then call a gobbler right into the other hunter's line of sight. The result is usually a successful kill. When it comes to turkey hunting, there are a vast number of tips, tricks and advice for getting results. As with many other things, what works for one hunter does not always work for another. However, sticking with the basics has always been a good rule of thumb when it comes to turkey hunting.

Turkey Hunting Basics

Many hunters like to test their skill at bringing home their own wild turkey for dinner. While it is a fun and exciting hunt, it can also be a challenging and tiring one. Turkey season is often offered in both the spring and the fall; this will give hunters a chance at turkey a few times a year. Tactics are different for both the spring and the fall hunt though, so with a little bit of time and research a hunter can step out into the woods confident that he's acquired all the tools to bag a trophy gobbler.

Scouting your local area for popular turkey haunts is an important part of planning a turkey hunt. Many hunters make a point to do this outside of turkey season so they can get an idea of the habits of the turkeys in their area. For the sake of practice, many hunters also like to use a call when scouting areas outside of turkey season. This will allow the hunter to perfect his call by the time season comes around. When practicing your call with real turkeys though, it's important to listen for their habits when gobbling. It doesn't take much for a turkey to grow tired of too much gobbling and move out of the area.

Because there are two turkey seasons many hunters like to switch up their game plan. Turkeys are smart creatures and often grow wise to the hunter's tactics. In the spring of the year when males are trying to mate with as many females as possible, they are much more interested in investigating every call a hunter may make. In the fall, however, when mating season is past its peak, it can be more difficult to call turkeys in with calls. Instead of using a mating call, many hunters try to mimic the turkeys; for instance aggressive calls should be met with aggressive calls and soft calls with soft ones.

Another great thing many hunters like to use is the help of another hunter. For instance, with two hunters properly positioned a few yards apart, one hunter can call in a gobbler right into the other hunter's line of sight. When it comes to turkey hunting there are a number of tips and tricks hunters like to use, but the key is also to practice your game even in the off-season. The hunter who knows more about his target will have a more successful hunt.

The Many Types Of Hunting Dogs

Hunting dogs are here to assist the hunter, and these dogs have slowly evolved into many different types of hunting dogs' such as the general hunting dogs; sporting or gun dogs; or scent hounds. The origin of today's gun dog breeds began back in the 1400s to 1600s in Western Europe. The dogs used during this time were the Pointers, for locating game. And as more and more guns were begun to be used for hunting, other types of hunting dogs that developed were the flushing setter and spaniel breeds.

Over time, especially in England, to go on a hunt may require many different types of hunting dogs' pointing and flushing hunting dogs located game in the surrounding brush; the wind hounds coursed it down; terriers went underground after the game if it went into the burrows; and the scent hounds tracked it down if it ran across country. But over time, the hunt simplified itself, with the sporting dogs maintaining a wide tolerance of people and little territoriality due to the fact they are mostly used by non-owners for hunting. A high tolerance for other dogs and people are almost a needed requirement for hunting dogs. If the owner has a hunting lodge or some form of hunting business that hires hunting dogs out, that dog has to obey commands and go hunting for a stranger as if that person is their owner.

These types of hunting dogs to not growl or show signs of aggression toward their hunted prey, because this would be a behavior that would scare the prey away instead of catching it. Instead, the behavior is of silent intenseness, to allow for the catch. Other types of skills and behavior demonstrate what the types of hunting dogs do over another' the scent hounds on their leashes can pick up tracks and scents that other days may miss, one that is many days old. On the other hand, a good pointer can point and freeze birds that assume they are well hidden from view, whole the popular retrievers can retrieve birds in freezing water all day long. This is a lot different than England's many steps of different birds for hunting.

So, the types of hunting dogs have changed a lot over the years and from one country over another. And then, of course, different countries breed different hunting dogs for hunting different types of game birds in their country. Some hunters will travel overseas to hunt, while others prefer to hunt in their back yard, so knowing these differences will make a difference.

The Hunting Dog Deconstructed

Hunter and hunting dog have developed over centuries to form a harmonious relationship and strong bond. The dog was domesticated for the sole purpose of aiding early man in finding food for survival. Because of man's reliance on this animal, an unbreakable loyalty was formed that still exists today. Over time the different breeds developed to serve different purposes; as watchdogs, herders, and for hunting. The groups generally referred to are the general hunting dog, the sporting or gun dog, and the scent hounds.

The origin of today's gun dog began as early as the 15th century in Western Europe. The dogs used at this time were pointers, who located game for their owners. As time passed other breeds developed to include the flushing setter and the spaniels.

Over the years different breeds were bred for different characteristics, all to aid the hunter in catching game. The pointing and flushing dogs located game; the wind hounds coursed it down; terriers went underground after the game; and the scent hounds tracked it down if it ran across country. Because of the fierce loyalty of the these hunting dogs, and their superior and friendly personalities, many dogs in the sporting group today are used at hunting lodges by professional services for hunters. These dogs take commands well from people not their owners and are very trustworthy.

Important characteristics of these hunting dogs are their high tolerance for all people, including strangers. Hunting today has become a pastime practiced by many people; the dog will not only come across many strangers, but also many other hunting dogs, so he needs to be trusted in these situations. Another important asset of the hunting dog is restraint. While hunting dogs are notoriously high energy, many have the ability to focus when on the hunt. Being quiet is often the most important characteristic while in the field, and having a dog that can't recognize that will only botch a hunting trip.

Choosing the right dog for the hunt is important. Scent hounds are able to pick up a scent on the ground a day old; pointers are able to locate game and freeze until the hunter is able to get into position. These dogs have been bred for centuries for their job, so trying to force a dog to be what he is not will never work. With a little research a hunter can choose the perfect dog for his hunt and enjoy many years of enjoyment with his four-legged companion.

Keep Ten Points In Mind When Purchasing A Goose Hunting Blind!

Summary: Anyone who goes on a hunting trip would wish to come back with a good haul and pleasant memories. Selecting the right goose hunting blinds will ensure the same!

Geese are extremely sensitive birds! The slightest disturbance, an unfamiliar sound, a noticeable change in the surrounding environment' and they are off before you can say cheese ! It is therefore crucial to conceal yourself and the goose hunting blind so well that they seem to be a natural part of the environment around the body of water or fields where the geese are expected to land.

Here is some handy advice on the points to be kept in mind when purchasing a goose hunting blind'

(1) If it is your first time, spend some time on investigation. Talk to the right people and consider all aspects before buying one. Do not employ a 'love at first sight' attitude or grudge spending a little more; you may have cause to regret later should the hunting trip prove a failure!

(2) You do not have a lot of time to set up your equipment. So go for something that can be set up as well as taken down with ease. A model which can be put up with the help of simple snapping or telescoping aluminum frame pieces is a good one. This is important as the blind is generally set up when dusk is approaching or even in total darkness.

(3) A lightweight goose hunting blind is easy to carry and easy to manage, but can get damaged easily. The choice is left to you.

(4) The blind should conceal you completely. At the same time, you should be able to get a shot at the geese without anything blocking your view of them.

(5) The sizes of the blinds vary according to the number of hunters' single, a pair, or a large group? A too small blind would cause the person to feel totally cramped and uncomfortable, especially if the wait is going to be a long one. Similarly, hikers would find it difficult to carry

large blinds with them. Finally, neither too small nor too large can be considered to be entirely safe. So assess the situation and make a wise choice.

(6) You may wish your hunting dogs to accompany you, if the area you are heading for is open fields. Then, the goose hunting blind has to be big enough to accommodate the dogs too.

(7) Long waiting periods can be made more comfortable with the addition of a propane cooking stove to prepare hot coffee or even a small space heater! Then consider a goose hunting blind which can accommodate additional equipment and also prevent fire hazards.

(8) Imagine settling down on damp or wet soil or muddy fields while waiting for the geese to come! The very thought makes you feel 'chilled'! Your goose hunting blind should have a solid bottom to prevent seepage of ground moisture. Whenever necessary, you can use it as a towing sled to move your gear to the water body or fields.

(9) The roof of the blind should be easy and quick to open, not difficult and slow. Even the best of camouflaging will serve no purpose then.

(10) There are new models on the market. Some large-sized goose hunting blinds will enable you or your group to shoot while seated on swiveling stools or chairs. This can prove useful if the hunt is to be extended for a greater period of time.

Download 100+ Books
Completely Free!
No Hassles...
No Charges...
Just Click And Download
100% Free!
CLICK HERE

This Product Is Brought To You By